A CAMBRIDGE TOPIC BOOK

The Automobile

Arthur N. Evans

Published in cooperation with Cambridge University Press
Lerner Publications Company, Minneapolis

opposite: *Ford cars and trucks then and now: (left) Model T Touring car, 1909; Continental, 1982; (right) Model T Truck, 1917; Ford Ranger, 1983.*

LIBRARY OF CONGRESS CATALOGING IN PUBLICATION DATA

Evans, Arthur N.
The automobile.

(A Cambridge topic book)
Previously published as: The motor car. 1983.
Includes index.
Summary: Traces the history of the automobile from the eighteenth-century steam carriage of Nicholas Cugnot to the modern motor age with its energy crises.
1. Automobiles—History—Juvenile literature.
[1. Automobiles—History] I. Title.
TL147.E93 1985   629.2′222′09   84-14380
ISBN 0-8225-1232-7 (lib. bdg.)

This edition first published 1985 by Lerner Publications Company by permission of Cambridge University Press.

Original edition copyright © 1983 by Cambridge University Press
as part of *The Cambridge Introduction to the History of Mankind: Topic Book*
under the title *The Motor Car.*

International Standard Book Number: 0-8225-1232-7
Library of Congress Catalog Card Number: 84-14380

Manufactured in the United States of America

This edition is available exclusively from:
Lerner Publications Company, 241 First Avenue North, Minneapolis, Minnesota 55401

2 3 4 5 6 7 8 9 10 93 92 91 90 89 88 87 86

Contents

1 **The horseless carriage, 1769–1885** *p.4*
The steam carriage *p.4*
Problems facing mechanized
road transportation *p.5*
The birth of the automobile *p.6*
Gasoline *p.9*

2 **The years of development, 1885–1918** *p.10*
Continental Europe *p.10*
The United States of America *p.16*
Britain *p.20*
The automobile throughout the world *p.26*
World War I *p.27*

3 **The years of expansion, 1918–1945** *p.28*
Wartime effects on the automobile *p.28*
The first British "popular" cars *p.30*
A new way of making automobiles *p.32*
Car and society in the twenties and thirties *p.33*
The Great Depression *p.36*
World War II *p.38*

4 **The automobile age, 1945–1980** *p.39*
Continental Europe *p.39*
Britain *p.39*
The United States of America *p.42*
The rise of the Japanese car industry *p.42*
"A mixed blessing": car and society since the war *p.43*
Towards the ideal car *p.46*
The energy crisis *p.48*

Index *p.49*
Acknowledgments *p.51*

1   The horseless carriage, 1769–1885

The steam carriage

Only a hundred years ago, the world had never seen an auto-mobile. Today, millions of them throng roads the world over. The history of how and why this happened begins with the fascinating story of men from many different countries who dreamed of horseless transport.

A self-propelled vehicle had been thought of as long ago as 1649 when some German clockmakers applied the idea of the clock spring to a small carriage. It had a spring that enabled the vehicle to move short distances, but it had to be wound up every few minutes like a clockwork toy.

During the Industrial Revolution of the eighteenth and nineteenth centuries, Britain was "the workshop of the world." The country's wealth in coal helped those enterprising pioneers who found that steam power was the most effective means of working machines in factories.

Steam power made Britain a busy, industrial country, and it also provided an opportunity to further the early ideas of horseless transport. If steam could power a stationary machine, might it not work with a machine that could move?

It was, however, a French army officer who first showed that it could. In 1769, Nicholas Cugnot built a three-wheeled wooden carriage that he called a Cabriot. It was more than 25 feet long by 8 feet wide (8 meters long and 2.5 meters wide). At the front was a boiler, a large metal drum holding water. When heated by burning coal, the boiling water gave off steam that pushed an iron rod attached to a disk (called the piston) along a thin tube (called the cylinder). Two pistons were attached to the Cabriot's front wheel by rods, and, as they moved up and down the two cylinders, the wheel turned slowly round. The Cabriot reached almost 2 miles (3.2 kilometers) an hour, but Cugnot had to restoke the boiler every 15 minutes. Even worse, the weight of the large boiler made the Cabriot clumsy and difficult to balance. Cugnot lost control of the carriage; it crashed and was completely destroyed.

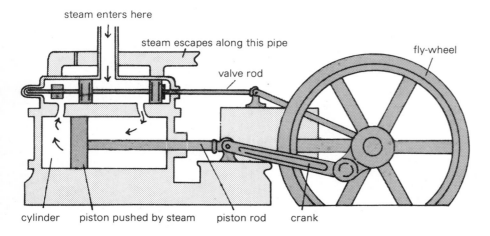

steam enters here
steam escapes along this pipe
valve rod
fly-wheel
cylinder   piston pushed by steam   piston rod   crank

In the earliest steam engines, the steam was fed into a long, strong tube (the cylinder) that contained a movable rod and piston. The steam pushed the piston along the cylinder before escaping through a hole, whereupon the piston returned ready to be blown along the cylinder again. The piston was linked by the rod to a crank which turned a wheel.

Cugnot gave up his experiments and returned to military engineering, but his Cabriot was the first milestone in the history of mechanized transportation. It demonstrated that steam power was capable of propelling a carriage, and quite a heavy one too.

The idea of carriages powered by steam was developed by other men in France, Britain, and America. They improved on the weaknesses of Cugnot's Cabriot, building smaller boilers that were lighter and more stable and needed stoking less frequently. By the early years of the nineteenth century, steam carriages were running regular passenger services in the larger towns of these countries.

In 1801, Philippe Lebon, a French scientist, invented an engine that was powered not by steam but by a mixture of air and coal gas. This mixture was ignited in the cylinder, and the resulting gas explosion pushed the piston forward. In 1804, however, Lebon was murdered, and this new type of engine had to wait another 50 years before its development was continued.

Problems facing mechanized road transportation

Tollbooths

Despite the promising start, steam carriages had virtually disappeared from Britain by the 1860s. This failure of early mechanical road transportation in Britain was due partly to the widespread opposition that existed to any attempts to reduce the importance of the horse and carriage and partly to the railroads.

Tollbooths charged tolls on travelers in order to raise money to maintain roads, and much of their income came from the companies running horse-drawn stagecoaches. They had no wish to see the decline of their best customers. The trusts were also genuinely worried about the damage that heavy steam

below: *By the 1830s, steam carriages were operating alongside horse-drawn coaches in Britain. This contemporary engraving shows one of Walter Hancock's nine steam carriages. These operated a regular passenger service in London between the city and Paddington.*

carriages were doing to roads, and they felt it only fair that these new vehicles should pay a high price to use the roads. Accordingly, steam carriages often had to pay tolls 20 times as great as those charged to horse-drawn carriages.

The first real bicycle fitted with pedals (above left) was built in 1839 by a Scottish blacksmith, Kirkpatrick Macmillan. The two pedals were linked to the back wheel by long rods. In 1874, H.J. Lawson (later a leading figure in the British automobile industry) built a much safer bicycle that had a chain drive from the pedals to the back wheel (above).

The Red Flag Act

A major blow to mechanized road transportation in Britain came in 1865 when Parliament passed the Locomotives (or Red Flag) Act. This restricted steam carriages to speeds of 4.8 miles per hour (8 k/ph) in the countryside and only 1.9 miles per hour (3.2 k/ph) in towns. They were to carry only goods, not passengers. They were not to exceed 13 tons in weight, and they were forbidden to cross many road bridges. Worst of all, the Act stated that steam carriages were to have a crew of three, one of whom was to walk in front of the carriage waving a red flag to warn oncoming travelers of the "dangerous" vehicle that was approaching.

Opposition to steam carriages came from farmers, landowners, and ordinary travelers who found that they were dirty and noisy and frightening to people and animals alike. Their disappearance was not mourned by many.

The steam engine was dirty, heavy, and wasteful. It took a long time to start up and needed constant stoking. The pioneers of steam transportation had not been defeated, however, simply diverted. The steam carriage had taken to the rails and grown into the train, which had killed off the horsedrawn stagecoach even before the Red Flag Act. Nevertheless, this delay in continuing the early development of mechanized road transportation meant that Britain made a late start in developing the automobile. On the Continent and in America, ideas for developing mechanized road transportation grew and prospered.

The birth of the automobile

The bicycle

In 1839, Kirkpatrick Macmillan built the world's first real bicycle, and it was soon followed by many others, most of them British-made. By the early 1860s, the ribbon trade of Coventry was in decline, and the prospect of any new trade was very welcome. It came in 1865 when James Starley, who worked for the Coventry Sewing Machine Company, built a bicycle in his spare time. The company decided to start up in this new trade, and it became the Swift Cycle Company.

Other men began to build bicycles, George Singer of Coventry and Thomas Humber of Beeston among them. The Birmingham Small Arms Company produced BSA bicycles. In 1885, James Starley set up in business with a partner, William Sutton. Their bicycle company bore a name which remains with the present-day automobile: Rover.

In Britain and France, bicycles proved very popular. They gave people their first real taste of freedom on the roads, and

Siegfried Marcus's second car built 1874–5, considered by many to be the first real automobile and still in working order today in a Viennese museum. It had a water-cooled four-stroke engine with a capacity of 1,577cc coupled directly to the rear wheels.

they were even used commercially for delivering small parcels. The sale of bicycles tended to be rather seasonal, with far more being sold in the summer. Bicycle makers, therefore, had time to experiment with other sorts of road machines, and in later years many of them progressed to the making of automobiles.

The internal combustion engine
The age of the automobile really dawned with the invention of a new sort of engine to replace the steam engine. In 1859, the ideas of Philippe Lebon, murdered over 50 years previously, were developed by Etienne Lenoir, a Belgian working in France. In Lenoir's engine, air and coal gas were sucked into the cylinder and there the mixture was ignited by an electric spark. The resulting combustion and gas explosion, therefore, took place inside the cylinder, not in a boiler outside it, so the new engine became known as the internal combustion, or gas, engine.

In 1863, Lenoir fixed his small engine to a little carriage and drove 6 miles (10 kilometers) through Paris at a speed of 5 miles per hour (8 k/ph). The engine worked well enough, though it was slow and low-powered. It could turn only a hundred times in a minute, and the journey took over an hour.

In 1862, a Frenchman by the name of Alphonse Beau de Rochas improved on Lenoir's engine by making the piston do four separate movements, not just two. The four movements happened so quickly that the series of explosions sounded more like one steady roar. Rochas' engine ran much more smoothly than Lenoir's. It became known as the four-stroke engine, and its principle is still used in automobile engines today.

Siegfried Marcus
In 1864, Siegfried Marcus, a German engineer working in the Austrian capital of Vienna, attached a two-stroke gas engine to the rear of a four-wheeled wooden cart. His horseless carriage traveled quite well at almost 6 miles per hour (10 k/ph) through the city before the engine broke down.

Marcus spent the next ten years involved in other projects, and it was not until 1874 that he designed another road vehicle. This was a wooden carriage with iron-rimmed wheels, to which Marcus fixed a Rochas-type four-stroke gas engine. It worked well, but complaints from the public about its noise led to police intervention. Marcus lost heart and turned from the horseless carriage to other projects, including stationary engines. Perhaps this lack of perseverance is the only reason why Marcus is not usually considered to be the "father" of the automobile.

The principles of the "Silent Otto" four-stroke engine were those of the present-day automobile engine. The piston made four separate, but very rapid, movements. The piston was connected by a rod to a wheel or wheels, thus driving the machine. This four-stroke cycle happened 50 times a minute. In a modern automobile engine, it occurs thousands of times a minute.

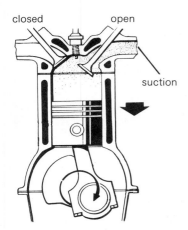

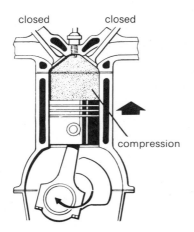

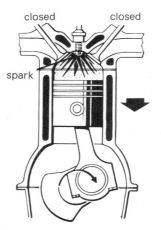

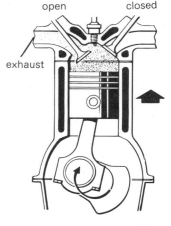

Suction: *The piston moves down the cylinder and the explosive mixture is sucked in through the inlet valve.*

Compression: *The valve closes. The piston moves up the cylinder, compressing the mixture into a smaller and smaller space.*

Power: *A spark ignites the mixture, and the explosion drives the piston back down the cylinder.*

Exhaust: *The outlet valve opens. The piston rises again, pushing out the burned mixture.*

Even better engines

The engines of Lenoir and Rochas were never commercially successful, but that built in 1876 by Dr. Nikolaus Otto was. Otto was an engineer in Deutz, a small town near Cologne in Germany. His engine compressed the gas inside the cylinder. The piston moved so quickly, quietly, and smoothly that the engine became known as the "Silent Otto."

In 1882, a German engineer, Rudolf Diesel, designed an engine in which combustion was produced not by a spark, as in contemporary engines, but by compressing the air in the cylinder so tightly that it became hot enough to ignite heavy fuel oil

the moment it was sprayed into the cylinder. This "diesel" or "heavy oil" engine was the most powerful of all internal combustion engines, and it was the cheapest to run. However, the engine had to be very strong and, therefore, heavy and though it did play an important role in the later development of commercial road transport, it was to prove unsuitable for most automobiles.

The pneumatic tire

The wooden wheels of most carriages and bicycles had iron rims. Rubber had been discovered in South America in the early eighteenth century, but only the more expensive models had solid rubber tires.

In 1845, an Englishman, Robert Thompson, designed a hollow rubber tire filled with air (a pneumatic tire), but its real development was left to John Dunlop, a Belfast vet. Dunlop was tired of the bumpy rides his bicycle gave him on his rounds, and the pneumatic tire, which he designed in 1888, was the first step toward smoother transportation.

At first, the new tires caused many problems. They punctured easily, and, whereas old iron rims pressed the loose stones of the road together, these tires tended to dislodge the stones and throw up clouds of dust. Nevertheless, pneumatic tires did permit faster travel, and in later years it was found that they were essential for speeds over 24 miles per hour (40 k/ph). They gripped the road better and were less prone to skidding than solid rubber tires. Dunlop's tires were sold by Harvey du Cros who later on was to play an important part in the British automobile industry.

The pneumatic tire was the main British contribution to the development of the automobile, but it was in France that such tires were used on a car for the first time. Tires made by the Michelin brothers, Edouard and André, were fitted to a Renault car in 1895. If the tires were damaged, they could be removed from the wheel rims and replaced.

Gasoline

The early internal combustion engines depended on a ready supply of coal gas, and they were used very largely for driving stationary machinery. The engine of a mobile vehicle would need a different fuel, one which could be carried in a small space and yet provide power for many miles of travel.

Crude oil or petroleum seeps naturally to the earth's surface in many places, and people had been aware of its existence long before 1857. But in that year, an American scientist called Ferris succeeded in refining crude oil to produce paraffin or kerosene, which was used as a substitute for whale oil in lamps. In 1859, in the very year of Lenoir's invention of the internal combustion engine, crude oil was discovered in large quantities for the first time in Pennsylvania.

One seemingly useless by-product of Ferris' refining process was a substance given the name "benzolene." This was to provide the other fuel needed by the early pioneers of the automobile: gasoline.

Development of gasoline engines went ahead in America, Italy, France, and Germany, and increasingly they took the place of air and coal-gas engines. The most successful experiments of all were carried out in Germany by an employee of Nikolaus Otto, a man by the name of Gottlieb Daimler.

2 The years of development, 1885–1918

Continental Europe

Daimler and Maybach: the first motorcycle

Gottlieb Daimler and his younger friend Wilhelm Maybach found that a mixture of air and gasoline vapor formed a far better explosive combination than air and coal gas. In 1885, the two men left Otto's company and set up on their own at Cannstatt. They began to design gasoline engines that were lighter and yet more powerful than those being built by Otto.

Intense heat was needed to explode the air and gasoline vapor mixture. In Daimler's earliest engine, this was supplied by a rod of platinum with one end inside the cylinder and the other end outside. The outer end was heated in the flame of a spirit lamp until the whole rod became red hot and the inner end ignited the mixture. This method became known as "flame" or "hot-tube" ignition.

Towards the end of 1885, Daimler and Maybach fitted one of their engines to a wooden bicycle, and Daimler successfully rode it around the streets of Cannstatt. This was the world's first motorcycle.

Karl Benz: the first automobile

Sixty miles away at Mannheim, Karl Benz was also experimenting with gasoline engines and horseless carriages. Some months after Daimler's motorcycle appeared, Benz built an engine that he attached to a tricycle. The automobile was born!

Benz was well aware that an automobile was far more than just an engine. Thousands of other parts would be needed. The engine would have to be started and stopped, fed constantly with gasoline, and prevented from overheating. It would have to work at a steady speed, even when the speed of the wheels might vary according to the steepness of the road. Brakes would be needed to stop the car.

One of the most remarkable parts that Benz made for his first car was a small machine called the magneto, whose job was to get the engine started. Inside the machine was an armature, an iron rod wrapped in insulated wire. When the car's starting handle or crank was turned (a pretty dangerous job, as it could spring back and break a motorist's arm), the armature spun round on a spindle. This generated an electric current

Gottlieb Daimler (1834–1900) and **Karl Benz** (1844–1929) never met, but most people consider them to be jointly the "fathers" of the automobile.

Daimler (left) was the son of the owner of a bakery and wine bar. After leaving school, he worked for a number of engineering companies including some in Britain. Returning to Germany, Daimler became technical manager of Nikolaus Otto's company in Deutz, making locomotives, bridges, and parts for paper mills.

Benz (right) was only a baby when his father, a railroader, died. His mother brought Karl up on her own and sacrificed a great deal to send him to a polytechnic school where he studied mathematics and engine design. He had a modest start as a fitter in a Karlsruhe engineering works. Determined to become a mechanical engineer, Benz set up his own firm in his late 20s.

above: *This curious looking contraption is the world's first motorcycle, built by Daimler. Two little "outrider" wheels helped give stability, and the small gasoline engine featured Daimler's "hot-tube" ignition.*

right: *The first commercially successful automobile in the world, built in 1885 by Karl Benz, is in a museum in Munich. It was little more than a flimsy-looking motorized tricycle. Nevertheless, it traveled quite successfully at 10 miles per hour (16 k/ph).*

that flowed along wires through four terminals. Each wire ended in a small device called a sparking plug, which was screwed into the top of a cylinder. Here an electric spark was produced, igniting the air and gasoline vapor mixture in the cylinder, thus starting the engine. This method, quite different from Daimler's, was called "electric coil" ignition.

On smooth roads, the electricity flowed as a smooth current. But on bumpy surfaces, the current was often interrupted for short periods, causing the engine to work in fits and starts. Benz later turned to generating electricity from a battery.

Another vital part of Benz's first car was the carburetor, a little chamber where the air and gasoline vapor were mixed before being sucked into the cylinder. It was Wilhelm Maybach who, in 1893, developed the most successful carburetor, the float-feed model. A metal float regulated the flow of gasoline that would mix with the air.

The moving parts of the engine in Benz's car needed lubricating to prevent damage, so oil was put into the crankcase, a large chamber beneath the engine. As the engine turned, a connecting rod dipped into the oil, splashing it throughout the engine. To prevent the engine from overheating, water was stored in a radiator and cooled by air drawn in by a fan. The cool water was then circulated in pipes around the engine.

Transmission, carrying the engine's power to the wheels, was one of the most difficult problems facing Benz and other pioneers of the automobile. Just as early factory machinery was driven by leather belts, so in Benz's car a leather belt drove a shaft underneath the driver's seat. Chains at either end of this shaft connected to the rear wheels.

The brakes on Benz's car were little more than metal "spoons" that pressed against the solid rubber tires. Suspension, which Benz considered vital for comfort and to preserve

the vehicle's life, was achieved through metal springs.

Having built one car, Benz built another and then many more. They were advertised for sale and were the first cars ever to be made commercially. It was this perseverance and public marketing that make Karl Benz the real "father" of the automobile, even though it was Daimler who had designed the first four-wheeled gasoline vehicle in 1886.

Orders for Benz's cars increased slowly, and by 1888 Benz had 50 men working for him. In 1890, they produced the four-wheeled Victoria, the first car ever to have gears. When climbing a hill, an engine had to work harder to maintain wheel speed. Many early automobiles could not climb hills; they came to a standstill and rolled backwards. Gears enabled the engine to maintain a steady speed while the speed of the wheels varied. To climb a hill in the Victoria, the driver slipped the leather belt from a larger pulley to a smaller one by means of a lever.

Benz's Velo of 1894 was more refined; it had three forward gears and a reverse gear. Thousands of Benz cars were built under license by other companies in Germany and abroad. By the end of the century, Benz's company was turning out 600 cars a year. However, they did not really change with the times. They remained simple, reliable, and cheap, while other makes of automobile became increasingly refined and powerful. Sales began to drop. In 1924, five years before his death, Benz was to merge his company with Daimler's.

The Mercedes

As Daimler himself grew older and increasingly ill, Maybach began to run things at Cannstatt. In 1896, the company produced the Cannstatt Daimler, the best automobile of its time. In 1900, Maybach designed another new car, the fastest, most technically advanced vehicle in the world. Maybach gave the job of selling it in France to Emile Jellinek, a German diplomat there. Memories of the German siege of Paris in 1870–71 meant that there was little love in France for such German names as Daimler, and Jellinek had to think of another. After much thought, he gave the new car the name of his 11-year-old daughter, Mercedes.

The automobile in France

The automobile had been born in Germany, but France was not far behind in its development. Many words still associated with the car today are French in origin: *automobile, garage, chassis, chauffeur, concours, coupé, grand prix,* and so on.

In 1894, two engineers, René Panhard and Emile Levassor, built a car and fitted a Daimler engine into it. For the first time ever, the engine was fitted at the front of the car, and its power was transmitted to the rear wheels by a long metal rod running underneath the car. It was called the propellor shaft, and, as it was turned by the engine, it turned the rear wheels to which it was connected. Most European car makers began to copy this "Panhard formula," and the automobile engine has usually remained at the front since then.

During these early years of development, the car makers themselves built just the chassis (the metal base of the vehicle that supported the body), engine, wheels, steering mechanism, and gear box. The car body, which sat on the chassis, was usually built by a separate coachbuilder.

In 1895, Count Albert de Dion, a wealthy French aristocrat, and Georges Bouton, a former locksmith's apprentice who had become a skilled engineer, together designed an engine that was twice as fast as Daimler's. They fitted it into an automobile that they built, and so began a long line of very successful de Dion—Bouton cars.

Armand Peugeot, one of the early French car makers, started out as an ironmonger and bicycle maker. This 1897 Peugeot's small Daimler engine was fitted beneath the driver's seat. As in most early automobiles, the driver and passengers in this "phaeton à dais" sat high up in the car. This model had pneumatic tires and good springs, but its brakes and steering were less satisfactory. Vibrations from rough road surfaces made the steering tiller very difficult to hold.

Louis Renault was born the son of a Paris button maker. He was a poor pupil at school and was finally expelled. In 1894, he and his brothers began building very simple automobiles, and fitted them with Michelin pneumatic tires. Their cars were also the first to use a power-driven rear axle with a shaft drive instead of driving belts or chains. This 1899 1¾ horse-power Voiturette had an unusual semi-circular tiller for steering. In later years, Renault was to become the largest car manufacturer in Europe.

Soon after, Louis Renault and his brothers, Marcel and Fernand, built an automobile in the family's garden shed, using the most simple of tools and equipment. They fitted it with a de Dion–Bouton engine, and the car worked well. They followed it with other cars and began building their own engines. The Renault automobile proved lighter than any other gasoline car yet built.

By the close of the nineteenth century, there were no fewer than 100 companies building automobiles in France. They were encouraged by the rise of long-distance automobile races, starting with the Paris–Rouen race of 1894. The first French Grand Prix (big prize) was run in 1906.

Steam cars were still being built at the close of the century. Indeed they were still more numerous than gasoline cars for they too had been greatly improved. They were often more streamlined and faster than gasoline cars.

Among the many early French automobile manufacturers were Citroën (who much later would mass-produce the first ever *traction avant* or front-wheel-drive cars) and Talbot. The latter was founded by an industrialist, Adolphe Clément, and his English friend, the Earl of Shrewsbury, whose family name was Talbot. Their cars earned a great reputation for style and speed, and, in 1913, a Talbot was the first automobile to cover 100 miles in one hour on the famous Brooklands racing circuit in Britain.

This first Fiat car appeared in 1899. The cutaway drawing shows the rear engine, the carburetor under the front seat, the rear-wheel drive, and the serpentine radiator.

Steam cars and electric cars, such as this Columbia model built in the USA in 1901, remained popular. In outward appearance, there was little difference between the gasoline and the electric car. Both still had the upright, "horseless-carriage" style. Beneath the body of the electric car were a number of batteries linked together. They were connected to a driving motor in front of the rear axle.

Other countries soon followed the lead of Germany and France. Holland saw the birth of Daf and Spyker. Italy had Lancia and Alfa, which became Alfa–Romeo when it was joined by Romeo, a brilliant young engineer from Naples. Giovanni Agnelli set up a car company in his home town of Turin in 1898. It was called Fabbrica Italiana Automobile Torino, better known by its initial letters, FIAT.

The electric car

An alternative to steam and gasoline cars during the late nineteenth century was the electric car, and once again France played a leading part in its development. In 1880, Gaston Plate invented the electric accumulator (forerunner of the modern battery), and Camille Faure adapted it for use in an automobile.

The electric car rivaled the gasoline car in Europe and in the USA virtually until the outbreak of World War I. It was easy to drive and very easy to start, unlike many gasoline cars. There was no need for the arduous task of cranking the engine with a starting handle, so women in particular found the electric car very attractive. It was also quiet, clean, and smooth-running. It could be fast too! In 1899, Camille Jenatzy, a Belgian racing driver, drove his small electric car to a land speed record of just over 60 miles per hour (100 k/ph).

Nevertheless, the electric car had disadvantages that eventually worked against it. The accumulator was heavy, and much of the car's power was used up in moving this weight. The accumulator could not provide "fuel" for as great a distance as a gasoline car, and it had to be renewed every three years or so. The car could not travel further than 40 miles (65 kilometers) without having the accumulator recharged, and it could reach speeds of 15 miles per hour (24 k/ph) over only a very short distance. With the introduction of the electric self-starter, the gasoline car confirmed its superiority over its electric rival.

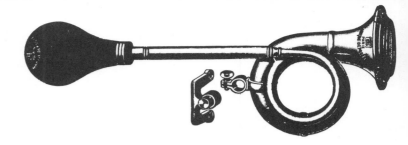

The adventure of early driving

During the early years of the twentieth century, car owner-ship gradually increased among the wealthier classes, and, by 1913, every royal family in Europe owned a car. For those who could afford it, the carriage, or body, of the car could be supplied by the coachbuilder made to an exclusive, individual design.

In its earliest years, the automobile was a luxury, a plaything of the rich and titled, but this gradually changed. Doctors took to cars on their rounds, and other middle-class people followed suit. Early driving was an adventure in more ways than one. Cars often broke down or ran out of gasoline, and flat tires were commonplace. Most early car-owners made sure they had a mechanic with them. The police also added to the sense of adventure by keeping an eager watch for excessive speeding.

Open to wind and rain, drivers had to wear caps, goggles, gloves, and dust- or rain-coat. Night travel, by the aid of kerosene lamps, was positively risky.

The United States of America

A warm welcome for the automobile

In the late nineteenth century, North America remained a vast, under-populated continent, much of it still untouched by the railroads. Outside the growing towns of the USA, the Wild West was still alive, and the horse and buggy was still a common means of travel. There was a great need for better transportation, and the development of the gasoline engine and the early automobile was welcomed eagerly. The USA was a rich land with plenty of raw materials needed for building automobiles and with abundant oil to power them. The rapidly growing American population, swollen by immigrants from Europe, quite soon provided a huge domestic market.

above: *Warning horns of all shapes and sizes were bought by early motorists. This "Kerry" special Treble Twist Horn was available in polished brass or nickel-plated.*

below: *This motor tea basket for four people, costing about $30, was usually sold together with a lunch basket costing slightly less.*

The Midwest, especially around the town of Detroit, be-came, as it remains to this day, the heart of the automobile industry. Here there was a plentiful labor supply from declining industries such as lumbering and bicycle-making. Engineering industries already existed to serve shipping on the Great Lakes and the farmers of the Corn Belt.

There were still forests enough to supply early coachbuilders with timber, and there were no steep hills to hinder early automobiles. Gravel deposited by Ice Age glaciers provided good road-building material, and there was local coal and oil for power. Just as important were the skill and perseverance of the pioneers who saw a future for the automobile in the USA.

right: *Charles and Frank Duryea left their farm in the Midwest, moved east to find better paid work, and took an interest in automobiles. This first car, which they built in 1893, was literally a buggy without the horse. Frank drove the car to victory in the first American road race, the Great Chicago Race of 1895. Of the six starters, the only other car to finish this race was a Benz.*

American pioneers

The first successful American gasoline-engined automobile was built in 1893 at Springfield, Massachusetts, by the Duryea brothers. Soon afterwards, another concern, the Apperson Brothers Automobile Company, was born. Elwood Haynes gave up teaching and became a superintendent for the Indiana Natural Gas and Oil Company, but he tired of bumpy rides in a horse and buggy. With the help of two local bicycle repairers, Edgar and Elmer Apperson, Haynes turned to the making of automobiles. Haynes and the Appersons were not the only early American automobile manufacturers to come to the new industry from other mechanical trades. Ransom Eli Olds had been a maker of steam engines; Studebaker, of wagons; Peerless, of clothes wringers; Buick, of plumbers' supplies and marine engines. Durant was a maker of carriages.

By 1914, almost 200 companies were building automobiles in the USA, and the list included names that quickly became world-famous: Packard, Locomobile, and Simplex (whose gasoline-engined cars had electric self-starters as early as 1911). No other country in the world felt the influence of the automobile as quickly and to such an extent as the USA. It rapidly became a normal part of the American way of life. More and more roads were constructed and played an important part in opening up the North American continent.

American automobiles were strong and reliable, and they tended to be much larger than European models. There were two reasons for this. Distances in North America were vast compared with those in Western Europe, so there was no market for small cars. In addition, the tax that was introduced on American cars was a uniform one, not varying according to engine size, as it did in Europe.

below: *A British advertisement for an Apperson car, emphasizing its quality and comfort. American car design had come a long way since the Duryea brothers' horseless carriage, but the Apperson Eight was one of the more sophisticated vehicles.*

Henry Ford

When he was 28 years old, Ford became night engineer at the Detroit factory of Thomas Edison, the famous inventor. In his spare time, Ford built an automobile and drove it proudly around Detroit. In 1899, he set up his own Detroit Automobile Company, saying

> "I will build a car for the great multitude. It will be constructed of the best materials ... after the simplest designs ... but it will be so low in price that no man making a good salary will be unable to own one and enjoy with his family the blessing of hours of pleasure in God's great open spaces."

Unfortunately, the company collapsed after building only 20 cars. Undaunted, Ford set up business again as the Henry Ford Company in 1901, but this too failed. The company was taken over in 1902 by his partner, Henry Leland, an ex-employee of Oldsmobile. Leland renamed the company Cadillac and began to build automobiles that were technically the best in the world. They were luxury cars in every respect, and it was several years before European manufacturers followed their example.

The fantastic success of Ransom Eli Olds' Oldsmobile Company, which was turning out 600 cars a year, prompted a Detroit coal merchant, Alexander Malcolmson, to "get in on the act." He and some other businessman financed Henry Ford in setting up the Ford Motor Company in 1903.

The Model T and mass production

In 1903, Ford built the 999, which became the most successful American racing car of its age, and for the next five years a variety of Ford automobiles came on the market. Late in 1907, Ford decided to concentrate on just one model, the Model T.

Henry Ford (1863–1947). Born at Dearborn near Detroit, son of an Irish immigrant farmer. He took little interest in farming, preferring to repair watches and farm machinery. Later he became a mechanic in a sawmill.

Production began in 1908. In 1909, almost 11,000 Model Ts were built, compared with the 65 cars Ford had been building each year so far. In 1910, almost 19,000 were built, such was the huge demand for the car. By 1920, almost a million Model Ts had been produced, and, three years, later the figure was over two million.

Olds did not stand still in the face of this competition. In 1908, he merged Oldsmobile with the Cadillac, Buick, and

The simple but stylish little Oldsmobile of 1902 with its sporty curved dashboard proved that body design was an important factor in selling cars. The Oldsmobile was an immediate success in Europe as well as the USA. In 1905, it was popularized in the song called "In My Merry Oldsmobile." It was not the first car to have mudguards, but they were included in the price of $650.

While Leland designed the super luxury car, Ford's Model T of 1908 was designed for the popular market. Indeed it became the most popular car in the world. Its 5,000 parts included windshield wipers, speedometer, mirror, fuel gauge, dashboard pull-starter, bumpers, electric lights, cape hood, luggage rack, and tool kit. Until 1903, European and American cars had the steering wheel in various positions, though usually on the right-hand side. The Model T had it on the left, and there it has remained on most of the world's automobiles. The "Tin Lizzie," as people called it, was simple but rugged and easy to repair if the worst happened. It did have its faults, however; it was uncomfortable and often difficult to start, and its brakes were not always reliable.

Oakland (later Pontiac) companies to form General Motors.

Nevertheless, the Model T was a winner, and, in 1910, with demand outstripping production, Ford moved to a new, specially designed factory at Highland Park just outside Detroit. Here Ford put into practice his revolutionary ideas about mass production of automobiles. He did not invent the automobile, but his production methods did make him the first to put the automobile within the reach of ordinary people. In 1915, the Model T, or "Tin Lizzie" as it became known, cost $560, compared with an average price of $1,700 for a European car.

By 1914, a Model T was coming off the Highland Park assembly line every 40 seconds. It was adaptable for many uses. Farmers had specially large wheels fitted to it so that it became a tractor, or they cut away the back and fitted a strong floor to create a truck. Ford called the Model T the "universal car," and he was right.

The Model T's technology improved as the years went by. It became the first American car to be built of vanadium steel (stronger than ordinary steel) and to have windows of strong plate glass. Ford realized that assembly-line work, where men never saw the end-product of their separate labors, would be boring and frustrating. As compensation, in 1914, he introduced the amazing guaranteed daily wage of five dollars for his employees, more than double that paid by most employers. No wonder men flocked to Highland Park looking for work! On more than one occasion, crowds of job-seekers had to be dispersed by the police.

The Model T is one of the major landmarks in the history of the automobile. It changed life-styles, working conditions, and industrial production methods the world over. Initially, how-

19

The assembly line was Ford's revolutionary idea for mass-producing automobiles. Each worker had only one job to do, adding one particular component to the car being assembled. The time needed to assemble a chassis was thus cut from 14 to 1½ hours. With savings in time and labor, costs were cut dramatically. This photograph, taken in 1913, shows magnetos being put together on a moving assembly line.

ever, European car manufacturers refused to take the "Tin Lizzie" very seriously. On the whole, they continued to turn out luxury models for a minority of people.

Britain

Britain joins the automobile age
Britain's coalfields had given her advantages for the development of steam engines, but conditions were much less suitable for the development of the internal combustion engine. The problems facing mechanized transportation, described in Chapter 1, dampened what enthusiasm there was anyway. Edward Butler, a Devon farmer's son, built the first British gasoline-engined automobile in 1888, but he never put it into production.

1896 was a busy year in the history of the automobile in Britain. That year the Red Flag Act was finally abolished, leaving Britain free to join the dawning automobile age. Thirty-three British and foreign drivers celebrated the occasion by

racing their automobiles from London to Brighton, and this race became an annual event in the British driving calendar. Léon Bollée of France won that first race in just under four hours.

British pioneers
In that same year of 1896, Henry Lawson bought the Daimler patents from a friend of Gottlieb Daimler and set up the British Daimler Motor Company at Coventry. It had no connection with the German company other than that initially it sold only German-made Daimlers. Before long, however, Lawson produced the British-built Coventry Daimler.

We saw in Chapter 1 how a number of early bicycle makers in Britain progressed to the making of automobiles. Those names were joined by others including John Marston (who started building Sunbeam cars) and William Hillman (Hillman cars). Not all early British automobile companies had their origins in bicycle making, however. Many began purely as car manufacturers: Napier (1899), Standard, Armstrong-Siddeley, Argyll (the largest car company in the whole of Europe by 1907, based near Glasgow), and Vauxhall.

Vauxhall
Alexander Wilson founded the Vauxhall Ironworks in Vauxhall, South London, in 1857 to make pumps and steam engines for tugboats on the River Thames. His successor, F.W. Hodges, designed a gasoline engine for boats and later experimented with its use in a car. In 1903, the first Vauxhall automobile was offered for sale at $730.

Vauxhall remained a small concern until the arrival of a 24-year-old assistant draftsman, Lawrence Pomeroy, who designed a much more powerful engine. In 1904, the company moved to larger premises at Luton and there, five years later, the Prince Henry appeared: the world's first real sports car.

above: *Lawson's Coventry Daimler of 1897 (no relation to the German car) was the first British car to race on the Continent when Lord Montagu of Beaulieu drove it into third place in the Paris–Ostend race of 1899. It had kerosene lamps for night driving.*

below: *As automobile racing, hill climbs, and rallies became recognized sports, so car manufacturers designed "sports cars" with specially tuned engines and styling to gain maximum speed. Vauxhall's Prince Henry car was named after Prince Henry of Prussia, an enthusiastic sporting motorist. It was a doorless four-seater with a V-shaped radiator fluted on the sides, a design that was to become a Vauxhall trademark. The Prince Henry could reach 72 miles per hour (120 k/ph), and it made Vauxhall a successful company.*

above: *The Rover Bicycle Company turned to the making of automobiles in 1904 with the development of this open two-seater with an average speed of 23 miles per hour (38 k/ph). It looked very ordinary, but later Rover models earned a reputation for attractive, high-quality bodywork. Rovers costing $1,020 each sold in large numbers. They were light, easy to drive, reliable, and economical.*

Society and the automobile

In Britain the term "motor car" was used officially for the first time in 1903 when the Motor Car Act made it compulsory to register and license all cars. Horns and license plates also became obligatory. License plates could be returned to the local authorities if vehicles were not used for a long time. The Act raised the speed limit on most roads to 20 miles per hour (32 k/ph). It had been 14 miles per hour (22 k/ph) since the repeal of the Red Flag Act in 1896.

The automobile had well and truly arrived on the British scene, but not everyone was happy. In 1910, a petition was sent to Queen Mary:

"The village women of the United Kingdom humbly beseech your Majesty to help us get some relief from the motor cars. We are sure your Majesty cannot know how much we suffer from them. They have made our lives a misery. Our children are always in danger, our things are ruined by the dust, we cannot open our windows, our rest is spoilt by the noise at night. If they could be made to go slow through the villages it would be a great thing, but we are only poor

Motor Fiend: 'Why don't you get out of the way?'
Victim: 'What! are you coming back?'

'It's stopped rainin', mister.'

people and the great majority of those who use motor cars take no account of us."

Unfortunately for these women, Royalty proved rather fond of automobiles, and later in 1910 the Prince of Wales (later Edward VIII) bought a Coventry Daimler.

The tollbooths had long since disappeared so a Road Board was set up to raise money for road maintenance through a tax on gasoline. Wealthy upper- and middle-class car owners were not put off. In the early years of the twentieth century, the automobile was a great status symbol.

Car owners found that they could live further away from their place of work, and towns slowly spread outwards along the roads into the countryside. Stables for horses were con-verted into garages for automobiles. Motorists could drive to the seaside, into the country, or to spa towns to "take the waters." Driving became a pleasurable pastime for people. It also gave rise to jobs that had not existed before, such as mechanics or chauffeurs (who could earn a good wage).

The automobile ended the isolation of rural villages and helped to bring town and country much closer together. Distance from a railroad station no longer determined accessibility. During the first two decades of the century, buses, mobile shops and libraries, even motorized clergymen, made a big difference to village life. On the other hand, old country roads had to be improved, and many an old landmark and fields and trees disappeared forever.

Early twentieth-century driving remained much of an ad-

venture. There was plenty of advice on what motorists should do in a time of crisis, such as driving in reverse gear up steep hills in case the brakes failed to hold the car!

These years saw an expansion of public as well as private motorized transport. In 1911, the last of London's horse-drawn buses disappeared. They had been replaced by buses built by Crossley, Guy, Daimler, Leyland, and other companies. (The electric streetcar, however, rivaled the bus as a form of urban transportation for many years yet.) They made movement for townspeople much more convenient, with the result that the suburbs of towns expanded outwards even more.

During the years before the outbreak of World War I, Britain more than made up for the late start she had made in automobile manufacture, and she was soon rivaling Germany, France, and the USA in production. The Automobile Club of Great Britain and Ireland, founded in 1897 with 163

Private car ownership in the USA before 1915

members, and later called the Royal Automobile Club (RAC), did much to encourage early driving in Britain. So too did the American Automobile Association, which started in 1902 in Falls Church, Virginia.

Rolls Royce's first car, the Silver Ghost of 1906, was so called because of its ghost-like quietness and its special aluminum-painted body. It became a byword for automobile luxury. Powered by a 7,000cc six-cylinder engine, the car could travel silently at 48 miles per hour (80 k/ph). This fine car came as an open tourer or, if the customer preferred, with a closed body. Note the four headlights, the wide mudguard and running board, and the sturdy wheels. The car's basic design remained unchanged for almost 19 years, when it was finally replaced by the Phantom.

The Honorable Charles Rolls (1877–1910). In charge of selling Panhard–Levassor cars in Britain at the turn of the century. A wealthy aristocrat and a considerable daredevil, Rolls had the time and the money to pursue various sporting pastimes; he was a racing driver and even an accomplished balloonist.

Henry Royce (1863–1933). Son of a Lincolnshire millwright who moved to London and died when Royce was ten. To earn money, the boy sold newspapers at a W.H. Smith railway kiosk. At 14, he returned to his home town of Peterborough to work as an apprentice at a locomotive factory. He lived with a railroad worker who taught Royce the use of tools in his garden shed.

Rolls Royce

By the time he was 20, Henry Royce was a skilled engineer who loved to make things as near to perfect as he could. In 1883, with capital of only $50, he set up in business in Manchester making arc lamps, dynamos, and electric cranes. The company flourished, and Royce turned his thoughts towards automobiles. He was so disappointed with a French car that he bought in 1903 that he decided to build a better, quieter one himself.

With the help of two apprentices, Royce spent the next six months building and perfecting a car to his satisfaction. Pleased with the result, Royce built two more cars. Their most impressive feature was their quietness.

Charles Rolls, London representative of Panhard–Levassor, was shown one of Royce's cars. He was so impressed with it that he decided there and then to sell no other make of car. In 1906, these two men from very different backgrounds, but with the automobile as a common love, joined forces to establish Rolls Royce. At Manchester and later Derby, they built the Silver Ghost, which quickly became a status symbol for rich people all over the world. Not long afterwards, Rolls died in an air crash, but the company's worldwide reputation for craftsmanship and quality survived his death, and Rolls Royce continued to prosper. Royce died in 1933, a year after being knighted.

The Morris Oxford of 1911–12 filled a gap in the British car market; it was a car for the middle classes. In fact, it was a good quality car at a moderate price, capable of traveling at 50 miles per hour (80 k/ph) and 50 miles (80 kilometers) to the gallon. Engines were built by White and Poppe of Coventry; axles, steering mechanism, lights, wheels, and bodies came from various other sources. Two independent sets of brakes were fitted to the rear wheels; one worked by a brake pedal, the other by a side lever. Unlike most contemporary small cars, the Oxford had detachable wheels, a great help to the motorist.

Herbert Austin

After emigrating to Australia as a young man, Herbert Austin obtained employment with the Wolseley Sheep Shearing Machine Company. He soon worked his way up to become branch manager in Sydney. Austin was a skilled engineer, and he saw the potential of the automobile in such a vast, sparsely populated country as Australia.

In 1893, Austin returned to Britain as manager of the Wolseley Tool and Motor Company. In his spare time, he designed an automobile, a simple three-wheeler, and soon followed it with another in 1896. This single-cylinder three-wheeler had independent rear-wheel suspension, a major advance in automobile comfort and roadholding.

By 1902, Wolseley was the largest automobile company in Britain, but in 1905 Austin left to set up his own Austin Motor Company in an old printing works at Longbridge, seven miles south of Birmingham. Among the businessmen who financed the venture was Harvey du Cros, who in early years had helped to market Dunlop's tires. By 1914, the Austin company was producing 1,500 cars a year.

William Morris

William Morris' reputation as a skilled mechanic spread around his home area of Oxfordshire, helped by his success as a cycle racer. By the time he was 25, Morris was building and selling motorcycles and repairing automobiles. He dreamed of building a car that would not compete with the luxury Rolls Royce and Cadillac or the cheap Model T and the sporty Prince Henry. He saw a big market among the British middle class, and his aim was to develop a car that would be reliable, efficient, and economical, with a wide range of accessories and fittings included as standard.

Morris began to put his dreams into practice in former stables in Longwall Street, Oxford. He had no plans or notes; he simply started to build the car and took it to pieces again

Herbert Austin (1866–1941). Son of a Buckinghamshire farmer. Loved drawing at school and went on to be apprenticed to an architect. Disliked this job and in 1882 emigrated with an uncle to Melbourne in Australia as an engineering apprentice.

William Richard Morris (1877–1958). One of seven children of a Worcester accountant. Moved to Cowley near Oxford and after leaving the village school worked for a local bicycle maker, adjusting chains and mending flat tires. At 17, he set up a similar business of his own in a shed with capital of just $20. Later became the richest man in Britain.

The automobile throughout the world

During the first decade of the twentieth century, the automobile spread from Europe and North America throughout the world. Even the "dark continent" of Africa was invaded by the car, for here Germany, France, Britain, and Belgium had many colonies where the influence of the mother country was strong. The British Empire in particular was world wide, with the result that the automobile appeared in all parts of the globe from Australia to Canada, India to New Zealand.

In "newer" countries such as Australia and New Zealand, towns and cities expanded with European immigration, and they were much affected in their growth and development by the needs of the automobile. In "older" countries such as India, where European penetration coexisted with an established non-European civilization, the effect of the car on cities was less obvious.

Mechanization of farming had a great influence on world food production. Parts of the Argentine pampas and the North American prairies were plowed up and became the bread baskets of the world in the 1880s. However, automobiles in the form of tractors certainly helped by speeding up and making more convenient much of the farmer's work. Other countries often had to change the entire character of their agriculture in the face of this new competition. Denmark's wheat farmers, for example, turned to dairy farming.

and again until he was satisfied. The engine was specially made for him by a Coventry firm. The car was completed in 1910, a small two-seater with green leather upholstery, spoked wheels, acetylene headlights, oil side and taillights, and a hood. At the front, Morris designed an unusual curved brass radiator, which was to remain a feature of all Morris cars for many years.

In 1911, Morris moved to larger premises in a former military college and an adjoining manor house at Cowley. With a workforce of 20 men and 1 office girl, he began to build more cars of similar design. He called them Morris Oxfords, and soon the company was turning out 30 a week. The principle of production in the Cowley factory was the same as that at Ford's factory in Detroit, but it was on a much smaller, family-type scale. Every worker had his own special job. Morris' brother-in-law, Bill Anstey, painted wheels up in the loft and lowered them down by rope when men below shouted for them. Morris himself delivered the finished cars to the customers. The Oxford cost $850, which was $195 more than a Model T but less than most other cars. Between 1910 and the outbreak of war in 1914, they built 400.

This 1917 tractor was typical of early models. Compare the metal wheels with features on modern tractors.

A Mark V "male" British heavy tank, photographed about 1918. The tank was not an adaptation but a specially designed war vehicle. It was a powerful machine, equipped with special gear and clutch systems. It could change gear quickly and turn around on the spot. "Male" tanks carried heavy guns; "female" tanks had only machine guns.

World War I

The automobile in war

In 1914, no army in the world had more than a handful of motor vehicles, though Britain and Germany had been experimenting with cars covered with thick metal plates, the earliest form of armored car. When armies moved way from railroad lines, most soldiers traveled on foot, and guns and supplies were dragged along by horses. Bicycles and motorcycles did prove useful, the latter especially for high-speed dispatch riding across the roughest of land. Some motorcycles were fitted with sidecars that carried machine-gunners; others were converted to carry stretchers for the wounded.

When war broke out, civilian automobiles and trucks were quickly requisitioned by the army. Though many ended up as rusting wrecks on battlefields, totally unsuited to war conditions, motor transportation soon proved much too useful to be neglected. In the early weeks of the war, the French used taxis and imported London buses to rush up reinforcements for the Battle of the Marne, which stopped the German advance and saved Paris. Automobiles as diverse as Morris, Singer, de Dion–Bouton, Panhard–Levassor, Daimler, and the Model T found themselves in action on all the fronts of Europe.

Trucks were fitted with searchlights, field guns, and radio equipment. Model Ts were converted into ambulances, staff cars, field kitchens, cargo-carriers, reconnaissance cars, and machine-gun carriers. Some were even adapted to run on the light railways that were used to carry supplies behind the front lines.

The tank

One entirely new form of vehicle appeared during World War I that was to influence future warfare all over the world. The difficulty with developing a large, heavy, armored vehicle was its weight and the fact that four wheels would not ensure satisfactory weight distribution. Tractors whose wheels were fitted inside caterpillar tracks to distribute the weight more evenly had existed in the USA for some time. They were ideal for work on soft ground where ordinary four-wheeled vehicles got bogged down. The idea of converting such tractors into "armored moving fortresses" was suggested to British army officers in October 1914.

Secret development went ahead, largely through the work of Colonel Ernest Swinton. In 1916, Foster's of Lincoln built the first such vehicle, nicknamed the "tank" as local people believed the new invention to be some sort of water carrier for the Middle East.

At first, most officers doubted the tank's ability in war, and they were not encouraged by its limited performances during the Battle of the Somme. As the war dragged on, however, the value of tanks became more and more apparent. In some places, they broke the stalemate of trench warfare where British and German armies had spent years facing each other from holes in the ground, each unable to drive the other from its positions. When the conditions were right, tanks could sweep right over trenches, smash through buildings, climb steep slopes, and provide cover for infantrymen.

In France, Renault began building tanks a year after the British. But by the time the Germans realized their value and began building some tanks that could hold as many as 18 men, it was too late. By 1918, Britain and France had several hundred tanks each and they, along with other motor vehicles, played a part in the ultimate Allied victory.

During the years from 1914 to 1918, thousands of men and women were trained to drive and maintain motor vehicles, and this was to stimulate further the world-wide expansion of the automobile.

3 The years of expansion, 1918–1945

Wartime effects on the automobile

The automobile in its various forms had influenced the course of World War I, and war, in turn, influenced the automobile. Defects that had been ruthlessly exposed in battle conditions were corrected. Car design and technology improved enormously during the "vintage" years of the twenties and thirties.

The war had stimulated demand among men and women for motor vehicles. Many of the people who had learned to use them between 1914 and 1918 were eager to possess vehicles of their own, either for business or pleasure. Many second-hand army vehicles were available for purchase. Moreover, car factories had greatly increased their capacity as a result of wartime demand and were ready to make many more cars.

Technology

Perhaps the biggest improvement in post-war car technology was the development of faster engines. There were two main reasons for this. New steel alloys and aluminum replaced cast-iron in the making of engines that were much lighter in weight, with aluminum pistons that could move twice as fast as old cast-iron ones. The second reason was the replacement of the old type of side valves in the cylinders by valves operated by a camshaft. This was a rotating shaft to which cams, or

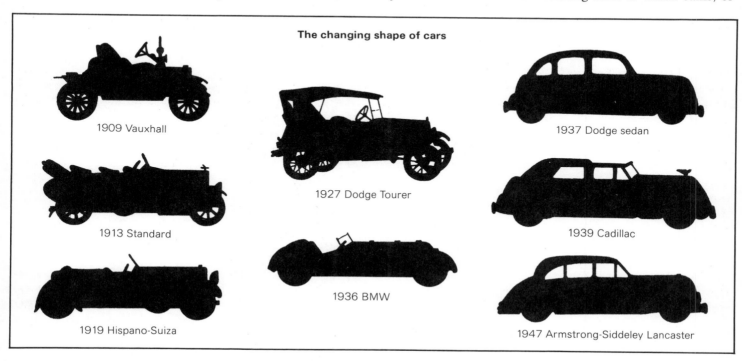

The changing shape of cars

1909 Vauxhall

1913 Standard

1919 Hispano-Suiza

1927 Dodge Tourer

1936 BMW

1937 Dodge sedan

1939 Cadillac

1947 Armstrong-Siddeley Lancaster

projections, were attached, opening and shutting the valves as it rotated. This allowed the gasoline and air mixture to be sucked more quickly into the cylinder. Again the result was a faster engine.

Shock absorbers and independent suspension became more common, allowing each wheel to move up and down separately over rough roads, giving a much smoother ride. Pneumatic tires became standard and had the same effect. Their life was prolonged by as much as 5,000 miles by the invention of cord fabric, thick-ribbed cloth fitted beneath the rubber.

Superchargers were developed. These were mechanically-driven fans that increased the pressure of the air and gasoline mixture and allowed much faster acceleration. Brakes fitted to all four wheels provided greater safety. Synchromesh gears were invented, making gear changing much smoother and no longer the nightmare it had often been in the early days of driving. The magneto, first invented by Benz, needed rewiring every four or five years. It began to be replaced by a more modern coil that lasted much longer. After 1918, dimming headlights were introduced to cut out dazzle for oncoming drivers.

In 1922, Daimler experimented with in-car entertainment for the first time. A radio set was fitted beneath the driver's seat, and an aerial protruded above the car. The driver could listen through headphones. The idea was some years before its time, however, as radios were not very good, nor were there many programs broadcast.

In 1925, cellulose, or synthetic, paint was used on automobiles for the first time. It was easier to wash and polish than the old types of paint, and it did not scratch so easily. Paint was now applied by spraying rather than by brush.

During the late twenties, bumpers became a popular accessory, but they did not become standard until the late thirties. At first, they were made of nickel plate. But with the introduction of chromium, they needed less polishing to keep shiny.

The late thirties saw further technological innovations: hydraulic brakes, which operated through liquid pressure rather than metal pressure, became common. So too did windshield wipers and turn signals.

Design

Automobile design also improved during the twenties and thirties. This can be seen from the series of small car pictures on page 28.

The 1909 Vauxhall was still very much an upright "horseless carriage" style, far from comfortable and wide open to the elements, except for the simplest windshield. The 1913 Standard marked a change to a more streamlined appearance that looked more stylish, gave better performance, and was more economical. The body was nearer the ground, though it still had very square lines. The hood was longer and the windshield slightly sloped to lessen wind resistance. Driver and passenger now had much more safety and protection.

The 1919 Hispano–Suiza, built in France and Spain, was one of the best automobiles ever built, luxurious and incorporating almost all the features of post-war technology and design. Its engine was derived from the airplaine engine that powered the World War I Spad fighter plane. It was not a mass-produced car but hand-made in small factories. By 1927, most cars were still open tourers. Some had a hood and side windows for wet-weather driving, but only the most expensive models were enclosed sedans. The body of the 1927 Dodge Tourer was still quite high and square.

Streamlining of cars meant the disappearance of the great protruding headlights of early cars. They were set back into the sloping wings, which themselves became curved and rounded parts of the car body. The 1936 German BMW sports car and the 1937 Dodge sedan highlight this trend well, as did the 1939 Cadillac Town Car. Outside running boards were incorporated inside the car, giving more room. Except for

The "bullnosed" Cowley, along with the Austin Seven, was Britain's answer to the Model T and was the first mass-produced British automobile. Most Cowleys were small four-seaters, but this is a less common sports version made in 1919. Its 1,500cc engine had a maximum speed of 55 miles per hour (88 k/ph).

sports models, most cars of the thirties were four-seaters. Luxury cars had instrument panels made from expensive wood such as mahogany and seats made of the best leather.

Better all-around visibility was an important advance on "vintage" driving, and it was evident in the 1947 Armstrong–Siddeley Lancaster sedan. This car also had an adjustable steering column to suit the driver. In most cars, the engine was brought forward over the front axle, and the seats were brought forward to the center of the car, giving greater room and comfort. This also enabled luggage to be stored in a trunk at the rear.

The predominant automobile color remained black. Accidents were frequent, and black was the easiest color to match. In the USA, Henry Ford claimed (or so the legend grew up) that he could supply any person with a car of any color, as long as it was black!

The vintage years saw the final break with the horseless carriage and the birth of the truly modern automobile. In 1922, there were 96 companies building cars in Britain, and there were 200 models from which to choose. These companies began to turn out more and more trucks as well as cars. Many ex-army trucks were sold for civilian use after 1918, and this was the way in which many hauling and public transport companies started up. Like automobiles, trucks advanced in technology and design, with more powerful engines, greater streamlining, and enclosed cabs.

The first British "popular" cars

The Morris Cowley

While large, powerful, luxury cars were still being produced in the twenties and thirties, a demand grew among ordinary people for smaller cars. This desire was strengthened by Britain's 1920 Motor Taxation Act, which taxed cars at the rate

of $4 per horsepower, the revenue going towards road maintenance. Insurance companies began to charge premiums on the same basis, so the advantages of smaller cars were obvious for the average motorist. Taxes were $165 a year on a Silver Ghost and only $75 a year on a Model T.

In 1911, Ford bought a factory in Manchester, and Model Ts started to roll off the assembly line there in 1915. Even so, by 1921 only 1 person in 168 in Britain owned a car, and the proportion was even lower on the Continent. In the USA, it was already 1 in 14. European car makers finally realized that if they were to compete with the Model T, they would have to copy Ford's assembly-line techniques.

Morris's factory at Cowley had been considerably enlarged during the war years, and it was by now the largest in Britain. The Morris company became easily the largest in the country, far ahead of its main rival, Austin. The production of Model Ts at Manchester led Morris to replace his Oxford model with a new one, the Cowley, which became the first mass-produced automobile built by a British company. Costing less than $760, the Cowley was immensely popular and did, in fact, outsell the Manchester Model Ts. Its quiet, smooth-running engine lay behind the characteristic "bullnosed" radiator. By now, Morris was an extremely wealthy man. He donated much of his fortune to charities, education, and medicine. As a result of this and his great contribution to British industry, he was created Viscount Nuffield in 1939.

The Austin Seven, introduced in 1922, was probably the most famous of all "baby" vintage cars. Like the Cowley, it brought driving within the grasp of the ordinary driver. Although basically a small four-seater, it could take mother and father in front and three children on the back seat. The Seven was produced in open tourer (known affectionately as the "Chummy"), sports, and racing versions.

I can't come out yet, Dear: 'I'm washing the baby.'

A 1920s cartoon from "Punch" with a typical joke about "baby" cars

The Austin Seven

Even the Cowley was too expensive for many people, and, in 1922, Herbert Austin built the Austin Seven. It cost $695 (later only $630) and was reliable and economical. Running costs were as low as under one cent a mile, little more than for a motorcycle.

Austin's Longbridge factory built over 100,000 Sevens during an unbroken 17-year period. The Seven was also built under license in France, Germany, the USA, and Japan. It became the first small British car to "invade" the American market. Technically, it was a superb little car. It was one of the first British models to have four-wheel brakes fitted as standard, and all its parts were made from the best materials available, including aluminum coachwork. Most coachbuilders in Britain built bodies for the Austin Seven at one time or another, so many people had a part in this wonderful success story.

William Lyons was one of those many coachbuilders. He started business in Blackpool in 1923 by making high-quality motorcycle sidecars. In 1928, he moved to Coventry, renaming his concern the Swallow Sidecar and Coachbuilding Company. It made superior bodies for the Austin Seven and for a number of other car companies, including Standard.

Just before World War II, the company developed its own sports car, the Swallow Sports (SS). It was very fast and stylish and became an instant success. By 1939, the cars were known as SS Jaguars and included sedans as well as sports cars. Later, just the name Jaguar was used.

End of the Model T . . . birth of the Morris Minor

Throughout the twenties, nearly half the cars made in the USA were Model Ts, and the Manchester factory was turning out thousands in Britain. But gradually the car began to lose its popularity. Designed for poor, pre-war roads, it was reliable and economical rather than comfortable and stylish. World sales fell behind those of the Chevrolet. By 1927, Ford was reluctantly persuaded to replace the aging car with the Model A. It was more stylish and comfortable, and it was available in four colors! It was one of the first cars to have brake lights operated by the brakes.

Morris' response was swift, and the very next year he produced the Morris Minor sedan. It cost $610, with a windshield of safety glass available at $10 extra. Within two years, the

left: *The 1930 Morris Minor shown here was based on the 1928 model. It had a fabric-covered body, which made the car light and fast, capable of reaching 65 miles per hour (104 k/ph). The car had a fold-down hood and a windshield of safety glass with a single wiper. The famous "bullnosed" radiator had disappeared.*

below: *This drawing shows one of the huge presses developed by Edward Budd and used by the Morris company at Cowley. A man pushed a sheet of thin steel into the bottom of the machine. The press crashed down, stamping the sheet into a certain shape (door, hood, wing, etc.). It then rose up again, allowing the operator to remove the molded sheet and insert another.*

price had been brought down to $490. One Minor achieved 100 miles per hour (160 k/ph) at Brooklands, and another traveled 100 miles on a gallon of gasoline.

The automobile industry was by now nothing if not competitive, and, in 1933, Ford responded with the Ford Popular. Built in Manchester, the Popular was the first Ford to be designed in Britain specifically for the British market. It did 40 miles per gallon and lived up to its name.

A new way of making automobiles

The building of the chassis and of the car body were, as we have seen, two separate trades. Every large town in Britain had at least one coachbuilder by now. The body was fitted to the chassis by means of bolts, and it was an extremely lengthy process. So was much else in the construction of a new automobile, where mass-production techniques were still a novelty. Painting the car by hand took at least three weeks. As the twenties wore on, car bodies became somewhat more standardized, though a wide choice still remained.

During the early part of World War I, an American named Edward Budd invented an entirely new way of constructing an automobile that did away with the need for a separate chassis and body. He built huge machines capable of exerting 2,000 tons of pressure on sheets of steel. These machines, or presses, molded the steel sheets into the required shapes: wings, hoods, floors, trunks, doors, and so on. All these molded "pressings"

were then welded (not bolted) into one complete all-steel body. The resulting car frame was strong but light, and, because it was all in one piece, it did not develop the irritating squeaks and rattles that often plagued earlier cars.

In 1927, Morris invited Budd to build a factory next door to his own at Cowley. The plan went ahead, and Budd's giant presses became the first stage in the Morris assembly line. Called Pressed Steel, this concern built all-steel bodies here for the next 50 years, supplying both British and foreign manufacturers. The German company of Adam Opel was, in fact, the first to use these bodies commercially.

Car and society in the twenties and thirties

The twenties saw the beginning of mass road transportation. For the first time, many countries, including Britain, emerged as motorized societies. The automobile industry was probably the most successful of all the industries that flourished in Britain during these years. This was an age of many lasting social changes, and the automobile can claim to have been one of the major causes.

Private car ownership in the USA between the wars

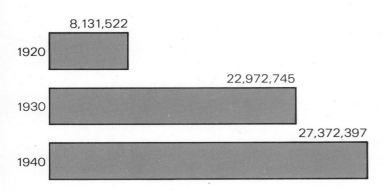

8,131,522
1920

22,972,745
1930

27,372,397
1940

Roads and road safety

During the twenties, roads in most of the world's industrialized countries became congested by cars, trucks, motorcycles, vans, taxis, buses, streetcars, and trolley buses. In 1914, London was the only British city with buses; within a decade, there were bus services all over the country, even in remote rural areas.

Until 1920, there had been virtually no long-distance road transportation; the railroad was still predominant. Most roads were still, therefore, more suited to the horse and carriage than to fast, heavy machines. Road engineering slowly improved in the early twenties, and asphalt became the principal road surfacing material. In 1923, the first of the American "highways" was built. These were wide roads with four lanes, no sharp bends, and few stoplights. Italy built similar *autostrade* and Germany, *"Autobahnen."*

In 1920, the Road Board in Britain was replaced by the Ministry of Transport. It classified the country's roads A, B, or C according to their width and importance, and the most vital trunk roads became the responsibility of the Ministry itself, though the others were still looked after by the local authorities. Even so, Britain was relatively slow in developing her road network. By 1930, the USA had built over 250,000 miles of new roads specially surfaced for cars; Britain had built only 226 miles.

The building of more and better roads did little to reduce the appalling accident rate in the industrialized countries, however. In the years between 1913 and 1917, an average of 6,800 people were killed in automobile-related accidents. This figure had nearly doubled by 1922. By 1945, the average number of US traffic deaths had climbed to an annual total of 28,076 at a cost of about 1.5 million dollars per year.

Although driving tests were not made compulsory for applicants for licenses until four years later, the 1930 Road Traffic

Act stated that you had to be physically fit to obtain a driving license. Third-party insurance was made obligatory so that compensation could be paid to pedestrians who were injured in accidents or anyone whose property was damaged. The police began to take even sterner measures against motorists. Armed with stopwatches, they timed drivers' speeds along stretches of road.

Road signs

To cope with the new automobile age and to help road safety, road signs become common. The Ministry of Transport in Britain recommended that local authorities should use red warning triangles with pictures mounted on top of poles to warn motorists of potential danger. Painted white lines appeared on roads in 1924, traffic lights in 1933, reflectors (to help night driving) in 1934. That year also saw the reintroduction of a 30-miles-per-hour (42 k/ph) speed limit in towns.

Leslie Hore Belisha, the Minister of Transport in 1935, introduced black- and white-striped crossings to help pedestrians cross busy roads more safely. They had poles at either end topped with orange globes, which became known as "Belisha beacons."

Even with more road signs and name plates in evidence, many motorists often had little idea of exactly where they were in the countryside. During the twenties, many road maps appeared in bookshops, and motorists were able to plan their journeys in more detail.

Towns

As public transport expanded during the twenties, so too did towns. They became much less compact, with further great expansion of suburbs and housing developments along roads leading out of towns. Small towns near large cities grew into "bedroom" communities, and, of course, the new houses needed garages. The roads between towns became lined with buildings until it was hard to see where one town stopped and another began. This new urban spread was too often unplanned, uncontrolled, and ugly. More and more countryside disappeared.

Improved rural bus services allowed villagers to reach towns more easily. The village store and the corner shop in the town continued to supply small, day-to-day purchases because of their friendly, personal service, but increasingly people traveled further to shop, usually into town centers. Here chain stores such as Woolworth and Marks and Spencer were found.

The automobile was more sudden and less predictable in its movement than the old horse-drawn carriage or the streetcar confined to its rails. In towns now you had to be alert to stay alive!

Road transportation: passengers and goods

By 1930, there were thousands of bus companies throughout Britain, some with only one or two vehicles. They often competed with each other on the same route, dashing madly along to win the race to pick up passengers. The 1930 Road Traffic Act reduced this number by dividing the country into 13 "traffic areas," where only those bus companies that could guarantee a regular and stable service were granted licenses to operate.

Hauling, bus, and coach companies could fix their own charges while railroad rates were fixed by law and were invariably higher. As a result, the railroads lost half their traffic to the roads during the twenties and thirties. By enabling direct delivery of goods from factory to shop, trucks played an important economic role, changing trading patterns and often cutting out the middle men.

Going to the races in 1920.
After World War I, groups of people, from church members to factory employees, began to organize trips or outings to the seaside or countryside. A new sort of vehicle appeared to cater for this need, one with a long chassis and a long body that had hard seats or benches running across it. They were called "charabancs" (from "char-a-banc" – "benched carriage" in French). As most outings took place in the summer, they were open, though later ones had hoods and side-screens.

This London United trolley bus of 1931 was typical of many that appeared during the twenties and thirties as alternatives to streetcars and buses. They looked like buses but collected electric power from overhead cables.

Employment

For motorist and non-motorist alike, mass road transportation completely transformed society. There was work to be had in car factories, car salesrooms, accessory shops, car parts factories, garages, gasoline stations, road building, and advertising. Buses, trucks, vans, and taxis demanded drivers and, therefore, created a large pool of employment. Wealthy families or businessmen often employed chauffeurs. It was a respectable job during these times — a regular, secure post with a smart uniform and often accommodation included and, invariably, a handsome luxury car to drive.

Industry

Roads began to replace railroads as factors in industrial location, and this new freedom led to the scattering of industry over wider areas. Mass-production techniques spread from car factories to other industries, enabling goods to be produced more cheaply.

Being an assembly industry, where thousands of different components were fitted together to make one product, the automobile industry stimulated the development of many associated industries such as metallurgy, engineering, electrical goods, machine tools, glass, rubber, paint, and oil-refining. They all made handsome profits.

Farming

The automobile age ended the isolation of the rural village and opened up a new era for farming. Trucks and tractors gradually replaced horses and old farming equipment. By the late thirties, farm workers needed to know more about engines than horse feed. Farming habits changed drastically. No longer did the whole village have to turn out to help with the harvest; farm mechanization lessened the need for farm labor and increased the rural depopulation and drift to the industrial towns that continued for the next 50 years.

Leisure

Credit buying boomed in the twenties and thirties and, together with the Morris Cowley and the Austin Seven, spread car ownership to the working class. By 1939, 1 person in 25 in Britain owned a car. Trips could be made to distant friends, to the countryside, or to the seaside. The first of Billy Butlin's holiday camps opened in 1937 at Skegness, attracting many families who could drive there. The car and the bus helped to make it easier to reach places of entertainment, and these years saw many more swimming pools, dance halls, and movie theaters opened. House design had to take into account the need for a garage for the family car.

Automobile racing, rallies, and hill climbs became popular sports throughout the motorized world during the twenties. At the Brooklands racing circuit in Britain, there was even gambling on automobile races. In 1925, racing was banned on public roads in mainland Britain for safety reasons, and the following years saw the opening of a number of race tracks. Brooklands had been built in Surrey as early as 1907 and remained the best known. Its banked track, the first of its kind in the world, permitted cars to turn at very high speeds.

The desire for speed went beyond mere racing. Huge cars were built specially to try to go faster than anything else on land. In 1929, at Daytona in Florida, Sir Henry Segrave in his "Golden Arrow" raised the world land speed record to 231 miles per hour (368 k/ph). During the early thirties, Sir Malcolm Campbell in his "Bluebird" cars raised it five more times, and, in 1939, John Cobb reached 369 miles per hour (592 k/ph).

Crime

Like any machine, the automobile could be used for good purposes or for evil. In the USA, particularly, criminals used cars to strike and escape quickly. Chicago became notorious for rival gangs fighting their battles with pistols and machine guns from cars. Leaders such as "Machine Gun" Kelly and

Al Capone had special, bullet-proof cars built for themselves, an idea that was copied by kings and rulers all over the world.

The Great Depression

The continued progress of the automobile

1930 saw the beginning of a world-wide financial and trade slump. Industry declined, companies closed, and millions of people were thrown out of work. These hard times of the thirties became known as the Great Depression. It seems strange that during years when almost all other industries were in decline, the automobile industry continued to thrive, but there were several reasons for this.

Despite the appalling unemployment, the standard of living and the real wages of those still in work rose between 1922 and 1939, and there was no shortage of customers for automobiles. In 1931, the British government decided that the British currency was no longer to be valued in gold. This devalued the pound, as compared with foreign currencies, so the British exports were cheaper abroad. This was quite an opportunity for car manufacturers, and they took advantage of it. There was a large number of colonies in which British cars could find a ready market. An import tax of 33 percent on foreign cars also helped their cause.

Despite fears to the contrary, oil supplies did not disappear during the thirties. In fact, oil fields throughout the world from North and South America to North Africa, the Middle East, and the Soviet Union were expanded and new ones exploited, so the fuel needed by the automobile continued to be produced. When world trade did begin to pick up again, it was the old industries that continued to stagnate. Newer industries such as the automobile industry prospered.

A further reason for the prosperity of the automobile industry in the lean times was that car companies set up factories

to build aircraft and airplane engines, using the principles of the internal combustion engine. In Britain, the RAF was expanding rapidly and desperately needed aircraft. As the thirties wore on, the automobile industry in Europe and the USA was already responding to the dark clouds of war that seemed once more to be gathering. Military vehicles were produced in increasing numbers alongside civilian ones.

Mass production made it impossible for small car concerns to compete with giants, and, by 1939, the number of car companies throughout the world had fallen drastically. Only 20 remained in Britain. Some disappeared without a trace; others were swallowed up by larger companies, including such quite famous names as Bentley.

Although large luxury cars such as the Rolls Royce Phantom and the Bentley still had customers during the thirties, it was smaller, cheaper cars that predominated. Sports cars too appeared in increasing numbers. The little MGs built at Abingdon after 1925 became the symbol of dashing young men in the "roaring twenties" and in the thirties.

Birth of Volkswagen

In Germany, one new enterprise was born in these difficult years with the help of government backing. Ferdinand Porsche worked his way up through the German automobile industry until he became chief designer for the Auto–Union conglomerate. Adolf Hitler, who became dictator of Germany in

In 1925, Cecil Kimber built a sports car out of assorted Morris parts. It became known as the MG (Morris Garages). This 1930 version was very light and fast, and the car became an instant success among sporting motorists in Europe and the USA.

1933, was impressed with Porsche's ideas of building a *"Volkswagen"* (a car for the people), and he decided to finance it as part of the Nazi Party's *Kraft durch Freude* ("Strength through Joy") movement. Hardly had Porsche been given the go-ahead for the *KdF-Wagen* ("Strength through Joy Car") than war broke out, and other priorities became more urgent.

Dr. Ferdinand Porsche (1875–1951). Born in Austria. Apprenticed to a tinsmith at 17, but his passion was for engines and automobiles. Shared Henry Ford's enthusiasm for a popular car at a time when most car manufacturers in Europe did not.

World War II

When the second great twentieth-century war broke out in Europe in 1939, civilian car companies throughout Europe quickly switched almost entirely to military production. The Germans had no intention of making the same mistake a second time by underestimating the value of motorized troops. By 1939, they had a great superiority in tanks and armored vehicles over the Allies.

The German Panzer (Armored) divisions spear-headed successful *Blitzkrieg* (lightning raids) in the early part of the war, over-running Poland, Denmark, Norway, the Low Countries, France, Yugoslavia, and Greece. The Wehrmacht (armed forces) still used a great deal of horse-drawn transport behind the lines, much more than the Allies. But overall, horses took second place to motor vehicles in this war.

At Wolfsburg, Ferdinand Porsche produced the Kübelwagen (bucket car) for general service in the field and the Schwimmkübel (swim-bucket), which could travel on land or water. In 1940, the American army took delivery of a general purpose (GP) vehicle, which became known as the Jeep. It was used by all the Allied armies for a whole range of military duties and proved to be one of the most rugged motor vehicles ever built. In 1942, the Americans developed the DUKW (Duck), a cross between a troop-carrier and a truck, which could carry men and supplies from ships to beaches and then overland. In the water, it was driven by a propellor; on land, it ran on six wheels. It proved its worth in the Allied invasion of German-occupied France in the latter part of the war.

Later in the war, the Allies owed much of their success to such well-known tanks as the American Sherman, the British Churchill, and the Soviet T 34. Allied superior military mobility and the fact that overseas supplies of vital oil continued to reach Britain, despite German U-boats (submarines), helped bring about the defeat of Germany.

The end of the war was not the end of the building of armored fighting vehicles. In 1948, Vickers built the Centurion tank at their Leeds factory. Bought by armies all over the world, the Centurion was one of the most successful and most feared of all tanks, and it remained in production until the sixties when it was finally replaced by the Chieftain. Military vehicles of all sorts continued to play a vital role in wars that broke out in many parts of the world after 1945.

The amphibious Schwimmkübel was a wartime product of the VW works. It was one of many vehicles specially designed for rough or varied terrain.

4   The automobile age, 1945–1980

The post-war years saw an enormous increase in motorization. Many Western industrialized countries, such as the USA, Britain, Germany, and France, became virtually dependent on motor transportation of all kinds.

Continental Europe

During World War II and for several subsequent years, gasoline was rationed for the civilian motorist throughout Europe. A few people went to extremes to keep their cars on the roads. Some taxi drivers burned wood for fuel; others cut their vehicles in half and substituted human pedal power for the engine! Electric cars that had not seen the light of day for many years suddenly found a new life, and gasoline cars were put away in garages or gardens to wait for better times.

After 1948, the Volkswagen factory at Wolfsburg, which had been destroyed by British bombs, was renovated, largely through the encouragement of British army officers. Opportunities to buy Volkswagen (VW) were rejected by British and American companies. Ford dismissed it as "not worth a damn."

Under the direction of Professor Heinz Nordhoff, VW prospered and grew to become the fourth largest car manufacturer in the world after the three big American companies. The pre-war plans of Ferdinand Porsche resulted in a car that defied the trend towards modern, sophisticated design. With its unique hood sloping right down to the front bumper, the car was quite ugly and became known as the "Beetle." However, it was incredibly sturdy and reliable and was to prove the most popular automobile ever built. For 40 years, the longest production run of any car, 20 million Beetles were sold worldwide, more than the Model T.

VW took over Auto–Union–Audi in the mid-fifties, and, by the sixties, Germany was second only to the USA in car production.

When economic recession swept the world in the mid-seventies, VW suffered less than most other car manufacturers because it had always concentrated on a small, economic car. Wolfsburg became a VW town, entirely dominated by the company, with apartments and recreational and medical facilities for its employees.

During the post-war years, there was demand not only for automobiles but also for all sorts of trucks, bulldozers, and other commercial vehicles needed in the physical rebuilding of many European cities. The assembly lines of commercial vehicle factories were as busy as their automobile counterparts.

Outside Germany, the post-war automobile industry was slower to recover, but Italy and France were soon making great strides. By 1961, France was making more cars than Britain, and over a third of the cars made in France in 1968 were exported. Peugeot and Citroën made many of these cars, the latter by having close links with the Michelin tire company. Renault was nationalized by the French government and became the largest industrial concern in France, making a host of products in addition to cars from ball-bearings to machine tools. In Italy, Fiat was easily the largest company and grew to be second only to VW as a European car manufacturer.

Britain

By 1952, 90 percent of British cars were being built by only six companies: Morris, Austin, Ford, Rootes, Standard–Triumph, and Vauxhall. That year, 11 years after the death of Herbert Austin (Lord Austin), the Austin and Morris companies merged to form the British Motor Corporation (BMC) with Lord Nuffield (William Morris) as Chairman. The merger was a sign of the times. Very few new automobile companies were established after World War II. Mass production had made it obvious there was no place for small firms. Fewer, larger companies meant there could be mass production of car

left: *The VW Beetle of 1948 had a rear-mounted engine that drove the back wheels. No power was wasted taking the drive along a propellor shaft. The small engine was cooled not by water but by air, which meant there was no water to boil in summer or freeze in winter. Unlike most car engines, the Beetle's had its four cylinders laid on their sides, not pointing upwards.*

left center: *The 1949 Morris Minor had the same name as the car of 1930 (shown on page 32), but it was a very different machine: one of the best small sedan cars ever made and one of the finest to drive. Millions were sold during a 20-year unbroken period. The four-cylinder engine could average 70 miles per hour (112 k/ph).*

below: *The 1959 BMC Mini became a byword for small car design and technology. Front-wheel-drive and hydrolastic suspension gave better roadholding than almost any other car. Sturdy, reliable, and economical, the Mini ranks with the Model T, Austin Seven, Morris Cowley, and VW Beetle as a landmark in automobile history.*

components as well as cars. Car models were reduced to a smaller number of basic types, and designs could be fixed for a good number of years.

In 1959, BMC's chief designer, Alec Issigonis, built the most famous small British car yet, the Mini. The engine was mounted sideways at the front so that the car, though small, was surprisingly roomy inside. The Mini gave Britain the lead in the world's small-car market.

In 1963, five years after Lord Nuffield's death, BMC merged with the immensely successful Leyland bus and truck company of Lancashire, which had already acquired control of Standard–Triumph. Overnight, the new company, the British Leyland Motor Corporation, became Europe's third largest after VW and Fiat. Its vehicle range included Morris, Austin, MG, Daimler, Rover, Jaguar, Triumph, Leyland, Guy, Albion, and Scammell.

By 1970, the other large automobile companies in Britain were all foreign-owned. Ford UK was an offshoot of the American parent company. General Motors had taken over Vauxhall and the Bedford commercial vehicle company. In 1970, William Rootes sold his family firm to Chrysler of the USA. Eight years later, the Americans, in turn, sold the British subsidiary to Peugeot–Citroën, who renamed it with the old family title of Talbot.

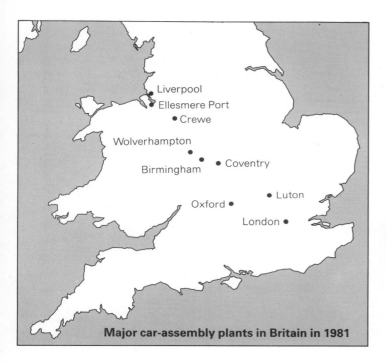

Major car-assembly plants in Britain in 1981

left: Post-war rationalization of the automobile industry, with the loss of independence of many companies, was matched by a geographical contraction of the industry. Its location in 1981 was an axial one, running from London to Liverpool through its heartland, the Midlands. The closing of the Talbot plant in Scotland in 1981 saw the virtual disappearance of the Scottish automobile industry.

below: The Austin Mini Metro was launched in 1980 in a bid to recapture for British Leyland the ground it had lost to competitors. Its shape was aerodynamically designed to offer less resistance to the air and thus give greater economy in years of expensive fuel. The MG name continues in this deluxe 1982 version of the Metro.

By the close of the seventies, only a few small, independent car producers remained in Britain. Rolls Royce's Derby factory was building airplane engines, and the car production side of the business, still as successful as ever but dwarfed by the developments elsewhere, was transferred to Crewe. Reliant built three-wheeled cars and the Scimitar sports car, and other small manufacturers, such as Aston Martin Lagonda and Morgan, built specialized sports and sedan cars.

Foreign and domestic competition, aging machinery, and poor industrial relations caused mounting problems for British Leyland during the seventies. Though its commercial vehicles and Daimler, Jaguar, and Rover cars remained successful worldwide, the company as a whole was barely solvent, despite heavy investment by the British government. The Jaguar E type of 1961 was replaced in the late seventies by the more luxurious XJS, and, at the same time, the Rover 3.5 appeared, the first Rover that did not have a rather upright, almost old-fashioned appearance.

Mass-produced sports cars were disappearing fast by the dawn of the eighties. Sales fell as insurance premiums rose and sophisticated Japanese motorcycles gained respectability. The 70 miles per hour (112 k/ph) speed limit and the fuel crisis of the seventies also spelled death for the sports car. British models were priced out of the lucrative American market. Sports cars became more and more comfortable but, at the same time, heavier, upsetting the vital power-to-weight ratio that was the essence of the sports car. Foreign competition from soft-topped models such as BMW, VW Golf, and Lancia Beta finally killed off mass-produced British sports cars. During 1980 and 1981, production of the MG, Triumph Spitfire, and Triumph TR7 ceased.

In 1980, British Leyland decided to go ahead with the planning of a car that would be built jointly by the British company and Honda of Japan at Cowley. 1980 also saw the launch of a brand new car, the Austin Mini Metro, built at Longbridge. It was the first major development from the Mini since 1959, and it was seen as the car that would make or break British Leyland.

The interior of the Honda Civic, a well equipped and comfortable car. Unrivaled production efficiency made Japan the major car producer in the world by the dawn of the eighties. In 1980, Japanese cars accounted for nearly 75% of all cars exported to the United States.

The United States of America

Following World War II, the USA retained its considerable lead as the world's largest producer of automobiles, a lead challenged only by Japan in the seventies. Although a few small, independent manufacturers existed, the bulk of American cars were built by the three big Detroit companies: General Motors, Ford, and Chrysler. General Motors alone had 60 percent of the American market, and, in 1978, it earned more money through its products than any other industrial company in the world, more even than the total income of some countries, including Saudi Arabia and Switzerland.

The rise in oil prices that occurred during the seventies led to a serious slump in the US automobile industry. The most fuel-efficient American car, a Chevrolet, did only 20 mpg; most did only about 14 mpg. Imported Japanese cars were vastly more economical to run, so sales of American cars dropped and production fell. In 1980, the best part of a million people in Detroit, directly or indirectly involved in the automobile industry, were laid off or were working part time. In 1980, General Motors made a loss for the first time in its history, and Detroit was a depressed city. The Americans had to consider the whole trend of their automobile history and began to think of producing smaller cars for the first time ever.

The rise of the Japanese car industry

Japan's post-war economic growth was unbelievably rapid. With Western help, industries began to flourish, and the road network to serve these industries was expanded. Austin did much to develop the infant post-war Japanese automobile industry, and a number of British and European cars were built in Japan under license.

In 1946, Soichiro Honda made his first motorcycle. Within a few years, he and others were manufacturing automobiles. In 1959, Japan put up trade barriers against the import of foreign cars and went full steam ahead to develop her own automobile industry. The Japanese were quick to copy and later improve on European and American methods of mass-production. Intelligence, good management, and sheer hard work brought rapid success. Thousands of trucks were built to aid industrial growth, and then thousands of automobiles. Honda was joined by other companies such as Toyota, Toyo Kogyo (Mazda cars), Nissan (Datsun cars), and Mitsubishi (Colt cars).

In 1952, not a single Japanese car was exported. But through the sixties and seventies, they poured increasingly into world markets, eventually threatening British, European, and American manufacturers. In 1980, Japan overtook the USA to become the world's largest producer of cars.

While Japanese cars of the sixties had tended to be somewhat old-fashioned in design and technology, by the seventies they were well up with the latest trends. By the end of the seventies, they offered excellent value for money, often being fitted with accessories, such as car radios, clocks, and heated rear windows, still unavailable as standard on many other cars. In the years since 1981, Japan has restricted her car exports to the United States at the request of the US government.

World car production

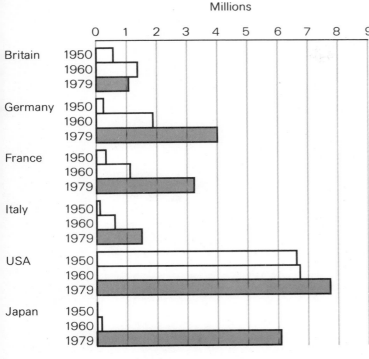

Millions

Note: In 1980, Japan's car production overtook that of the USA.

Car production in the USA—1979

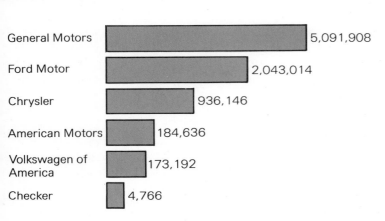

General Motors	5,091,908
Ford Motor	2,043,014
Chrysler	936,146
American Motors	184,636
Volkswagen of America	173,192
Checker	4,766

"A mixed blessing": car and society since the war

Leisure

Most European countries ended gasoline rationing by 1950, and, by the sixties, most of Western Europe was affluent and enjoying a high standard of living. Britain had "never had it so good." Car ownership grew dramatically and loan companies did a roaring business. Expenditure on cars tripled in Britain, far more than the increase spent on food or drink. The automobile became a symbol of prosperity, especially in the "swinging sixties," when it was said that "society had a love affair with the car."

People acquired more independence than ever before, and holiday and leisure habits changed considerably. Touring by car became popular, often to remoter areas of Britain and by ferry across to Europe. After 1965, trailer camping became a popular type of vacation.

People began to change their cars more frequently and not always through necessity. By the seventies, no one wanted to drive a car that was more than four or five years old.

Work

The automobile industry became vital to Britain's post-war economy and a good barometer of the country's success. By the seventies, 15 percent of British exports, in terms of money, comprised motor vehicles. British tractors dominated the world market, and British trucks could be found working in all parts of the globe. Export (largely to the USA), accounted for 75 percent of the output of MG.

Assembly-line work could be boring and frustrating, as Henry Ford had discovered many years before. But, in almost all the industrialized countries, it was compensated by wages in the automobile industry that were higher than in other jobs. In Sweden, groups of workers were involved more in the construction of the entire car in order to avoid this frustration. The groups performed a good many of the stages in the car's

left: *In this Fiat factory in Turin, automation has developed to the extent that there are few humans to be seen on the shop floor. Computers control most functions from moving car bodies between bays, as shown here, to spot welding.*

below: *Inner-city traffic congestion got out of hand during the sixties and seventies; though bypasses sometimes helped, they could not solve the problem. This 1972 photograph shows roads in London. In addition to private cars, there is a large variety of heavy load vehicles here, a reminder of the importance of commercial, industrial, and public service transport.*

assembly rather than the one solitary task, which was the usual rule. By the close of the seventies, some car-body assembly lines, including Austin's at Longbridge and some of the Fiat plants in Turin, were almost totally automated and computerized. Robots virtually took the place of workers.

Advertising

Making automobiles had always been only one stage in the total story. Selling them was just as important, right from the days when Karl Benz advertised his cars for sale. The advertising industry grew even more pervasive and sophisticated after World War II, and advertising was as important as engineering in the selling of a car.

The age of mass communication (newspapers, magazines, radio, television, billboards) provided many new openings for the advertising industry. As the post-war years progressed, advertising appealed to changing attitudes on the part of motorists. During the fifties and sixties, that appeal was to speed and style; by the seventies, the average motorist was more concerned with safety, reliability, and, above all, economy and value for money.

Towns and cities

Throughout the industrialized Western world, cities and society in general came to be dominated by the automobile and its needs. The automobile age saw the building of multi-story and underground parking lots, urban expressways, by-passes, overpasses, tunnels, and surburban supermarkets. In the USA, Los Angeles came to symbolize an automobile-age city, geared more to the motorist than the pedestrian. Ninety percent of passenger traffic there was by private car. Some said that nobody walked in Los Angeles; if you did, you risked being stopped by the police (in cars, of course) on the grounds of being up to no good!

Cities became clogged by traffic, and enormous jams at "rush hour" became a normal and accepted part of daily urban life. In 1963, the Buchanan Report *(Mixed Blessing: the motor car in Britain)* appeared, claiming that "it is not traffic movement but civilized town life that is at stake." One of its main recommendations was the separation of car and pedestrian by the building of "pedestrian precincts," streets from which the

The Humber Bridge, officially opened in 1981, took four years to build after many years of planning. At 4,653 feet, it is the longest single-span suspension bridge in the world.

automobile would be banned and where people could walk and shop in quiet and safety. This report was the first real threat to the progress of the automobile in Britain, unchallenged since the repeal of the Red Flag Act. In many streets, the parking of cars was entirely prohibited; in others, it was curtailed by the appearance of parking meters.

Other innovations during the late sixties and seventies were often aimed at discouraging cars from entering city centers. Public transport was given preference with schemes such as "bus-only" lanes and "pay-and-ride" bus service, whereby motorists left their cars in suburban parking lots and took a bus into the town center. One-way streets, computerized traffic flows, and electronically-controlled road signs were further attempts to solve the problem of reconciling the city and the automobile.

Transport and roads

Existing roads in Britain and other countries were improved and new ones built, often spanning wide stretches of water with huge, impressive bridges. The highway age came to Britain in the late fifties with the building of the Preston bypass (M6) in 1956 and the M1 London to Birmingham highway in 1959. They were the first roads in Britain to be designed exclusively for motor vehicles. Highways were wide and straight with relatively few access junctions, allowing high speeds. Service areas and roadside telephones were for the convenience of motorists. The economic recession of the seventies caused a

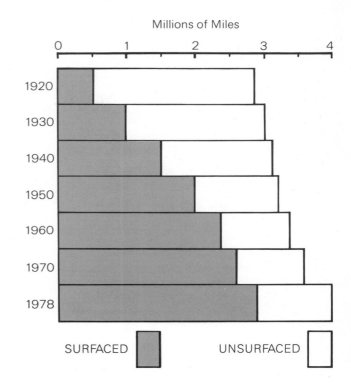

drastic cutback in road maintenance and road building in many countries, however. By 1981, the construction of new highways in Britain had virtually ended.

As roads became wider and smoother, trucks became much bigger and faster. "Juggernauts," trucks that shook roads and buildings with their weight, could carry huge loads at high speed directly to their destinations, right across countries and continents.

As heavier and heavier traffic took to the roads, railroads everywhere lost business. In many countries, the railroads had to reduce the number of trains, close down many stations and branch lines, and rely on money from the government to keep even their reduced services going. In some countries, the railroads tried to regain trade by introducing very fast trains on their main lines, such as the "Bullet Train" in Japan and the high-speed 125 in Britain. Although British Railways' advertising claimed in 1980 that "this is the age of the train," 85

left: *Pollution from cars became a problem not only in Western industrialized countries, but in the rapidly expanding cities of the "Third World." In Bangkok, a Thai traffic policeman wears a mask to protect himself against the poisonous gases of car exhaust fumes. Since 1977, the Thai authorities have stopped using such masks, fearing that they gave visitors a bad impression.*

Post-war technology allowed people to travel faster than ever before on land, though the highest speeds were attained in vehicles that were in fact not really automobiles. Stan Barrett's achievement in 1979 was in a rocket car with a Sidewinder military missile for extra boost, so the result was not officially a land speed record.

World land speed records

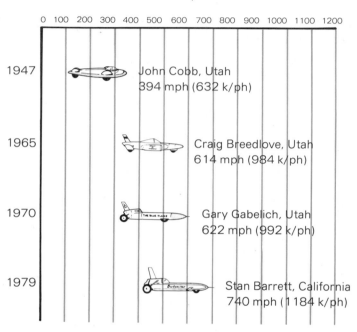

mph

0 100 200 300 400 500 600 700 800 900 1000 1100 1200

1947 — John Cobb, Utah 394 mph (632 k/ph)

1965 — Craig Breedlove, Utah 614 mph (984 k/ph)

1970 — Gary Gabelich, Utah 622 mph (992 k/ph)

1979 — Stan Barrett, California 740 mph (1 184 k/ph)

percent of all freight in that year was carried by truck, and cheap bus travel led to a drift of passenger traffic from rail to road too.

In 1968, there were 10.8 million cars on British roads, along with 1.3 million motorcycles, 1.6 million trucks and vans, and 100,000 buses and taxis. Road accidents inevitably increased. In 1968, almost 7,000 people were killed and 350,000 injured on British roads. By the dawn of the eighties, there were over 12 million private cars in Britain, and the government resorted to shock advertising to instill careful driving habits, in addition to the "breathalyzer" of the sixties and the 70-miles-per-hour (112 k/ph) speed limit on all roads, even highways.

Pollution

Countryside and houses disappeared beneath new roads and complex highway interchanges; some dwellings became uninhabitable. The automobile brought pleasure to millions of people all over the world, but at a price...noise, vibration, and carbon monoxide and lead in exhaust fumes.

Towards the ideal car

Automobile technology advanced still further after 1945. The fifties' and sixties' ideal of speed with style was replaced by the seventies' ideal of safety with economy. Research and de-

velopment made cars more reliable than they had been in the first half of the twentieth century. Improved aerodynamics increased speeds and improved fuel consumption.

The gasoline-fed piston engine of Daimler and Benz remained the basic type of automobile power-unit. In 1950, Rover experimented with a gas-turbine engine but fuel consumption was high and manufacturing problems great, so the gas-turbine car did not become a commercial success. The diesel engine was more economical than the gasoline engine, despite its weight, and gained in popularity through the seventies for trucks and also for cars. By 1980, most car manufacturers, especially in the USA, offered diesel-engined models for sale.

The 1951 rotary engine of Felix Wankel was the first internal combustion engine without the pistons of Daimler and Benz.

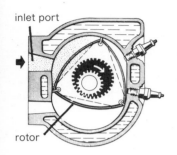
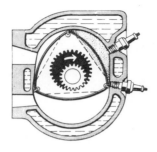
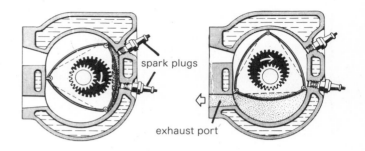

inlet port

rotor

spark plugs

exhaust port

Suction: *The rotor blade, like a piston, sucks in the air and gasoline mixture through an inlet hole or port.*

Compression: *The mixture is carried around and compressed as the space decreases.*

Power: *The spark plugs ignite the mixture.*

Exhaust: *As the rotor blade reaches the exhaust hole or port, the burned gas is swept out by the following blade, and the cycle of the engine has already started again.*

In 1951, a German engineer, Dr. Felix Wankel, built the Wankel rotary engine. It had very few moving parts. Instead of pistons, a triangular rotor with curved sides revolved inside an oval combustion chamber. One such revolution was equal to three in the ordinary piston engine, and the Wankel engine was smaller, lighter, and ran more smoothly. However, it was less durable. The small NSU company in Germany was the first to install Wankel engines in their cars. But after 1967, Toyo Kogyo, who used the Wankel engine in their Mazda cars, were fitting more of these than anyone else.

Electricity remained an alternative way of powering cars, but batteries were still expensive and heavy. The advantages of the electric car (quiet, pollution-free, not reliant on oil) were very apparent, and electricity could be generated by a variety of fuels. Some electric cars were built in the sixties and seventies, but, by 1980, very few vehicles, save for milk trucks, were powered in this way.

Alternatives to steel for car bodies were also developed after 1945. Glass fiber proved light, rust-proof, and cheap to produce but difficult to make in large quantities. Reliant introduced it into their Scimitar and Kitten (which they claimed was the world's most economic four-wheeled car).

Some Porsche cars were built of rust-proof zinc-coated steel. By 1980, the "hatchback" style was a popular one that characterized numerous British and foreign small cars.

Despite this advanced technology, 15 million cars a year ended up in scrapyards by the late seventies. Automobile manufacturers did not intend cars to last long, and, in any case, the general public preferred to change their cars at fairly regular intervals.

1981 was designated as the International Year of the Disabled, and this group of people was not neglected in the advancement of automobile technology. In 1981, Renault perfected a car that could be driven by people with no arms. Steering and acceleration were done with the feet; all other controls responded electronically to the driver's voice and operated automatically when the driver gave the word. At a period of time when car theft was a major and growing crime in many countries, the car was also almost theft proof. The doors opened and the engine started only when the driver spoke chosen phrases.

By the seventies, tough new safety and pollution laws were affecting car design and technology. Seat belts became obligatory in many countries, and the lead content of car exhausts

A juggernaut of the 1980s: this enormous hauling vehicle is moving heavy modules for the petroleum industry, traveling on the open road. While trucks and trailers can carry vast loads, they also consume vast amounts of fuel.

was often reduced. There were greater reductions in the amount of hydrocarbons, carbon monoxide, and oxides of nigrogen in exhaust fumes.

Truck technology advanced too, and comfort, power, and style improved as much for the truck driver as for the private motorist. Without motor vehicles (such as British Leyland's world-famous Land Rover) that could move rapidly over long distances and on poor or even non-existent roads, it would hardly have been possible to develop and hold together the numerous emerging countries of the Third World in Latin America, Africa, and Asia. The car, together with the airplane, has had a great social effect in almost every corner of the world. The desert Bedouin became acquainted with cars as well as camels; the Eskimoes of the Canadian north favored motorized sledges rather than the dogsled. In 1958, the New Zealand Antarctic Expedition reached the South Pole using motorized Sno-Cats. The automobile had come a long way.

The energy crisis

By the start of the seventies, people had come to realize that most sources of energy, oil in particular, were not inexhaustible. Even Britain's oil discoveries in the North Sea would not prove a lasting treasure. Wars in the oil-rich Middle East throughout the sixties and seventies added to the problems of supply. Oil became a political weapon in the hands of the exporting nations, and, at times, oil embargoes led to shortages in several Western countries. Motorists had to line up at filling stations for limited supplies of gasoline.

Gasoline prices quadrupled during the seventies, adding to world inflation and economic recession. The days of cheap energy were gone forever. Speed limits were introduced in many countries to conserve supplies, and, as we have seen, smaller, more economical cars became more attractive. South Africa, with abundant coal supplies but no oil, developed ways of producing oil from coal. In the USA, gasoline stations sold "gasohol," 90 percent unleaded gasoline and 10 percent ethyl alcohol processed from the corn crop. Brazil committed itself to running cars on pure ethyl alcohol derived from sugar cane.

Such developments were not a permanent solution, and the search for a new form of energy for cars proved a difficult task. Meanwhile, the number of cars on the world's roads was as great as ever, and the automobile remained for many people an essential part of life. This was not stupid selfishness; the whole pattern of life in most industrial countries had come to depend on the quick, convenient movement that only the motor vehicle could provide. It would take years of costly, unpleasant readjustment to return to steam trains and horses. There was as yet no alternative to the car. Nevertheless, the motorist and the automobile industry had been given a fright in more ways than one. They would never be as complacent again nor take the automobile quite so much for granted.

Index

accidents, 33, 46
advertising, 44
Agnelli, Giovanni, 15
Alpha-Romeo (company), 15
American Automobile
  Association (AAA), 23
Apperson Brothers Automobile
  Company, 17
Argyll (company), 20
Armstrong-Siddeley Lancaster
  sedan, 30
assembly lines, 20, 30, 33, 43
Aston Martin Lagonda and Morgan
  (company), 41
Austin, Herbert, 25, 31, 39
Austin (company), 30, 39, 42, 44
Austin Mini Metro, 41
Austin Seven, 30, 31, 40
Automobile Club of Great Britain, 23
Auto-Union-Audi (company), 39

Bedford (company), 40
Benz, Karl, 2, 10-11, 12, 29, 44
bicycles, 6-7, 20, 23, 25, 27
Birmingham Small Arms Company, 6
BMC Mini, 40
BMW, 29, 41
bodies, automobile, 47
Bouton, Georges, 13
brakes, 29
Brazil, 48
Britain, 5, 6-7, 9, 27, 33, 36, 37;
  early automobile industry in, 20-26;
  popular cars in, 30-32, post-
  World War II automobile industry
  in, 39-41, 43, 45, 48
British Daimler Motor Company, 20

British Leyland Motor Corporation,
  40, 41, 48
British Motor Corporation (BMC), 39.
  See also Austin (company); Morris
  (company)
Brooklands (racetrack), 36
Budd, Edward, 32-33
Buick (company), 17, 18
bumpers, 29
buses, 22, 23, 27, 33, 34, 36
Butler, Edward, 20

Cabriot, 4, 5
Cadillac Company, 18, 25, 29
Canstatt Daimler, 12
carburetor, 11
Centurion, 38
charabancs, 35
Chrysler (company), 40, 42
Citroën (company), 14, 39
Clément, Adolphe, 14
Colt, 42
Coventry Daimler, 21, 22
Coventry Sewing Machine Company, 6
Cowley, 30, 31
Cros, Harvey du, 9, 25
Crossley (company), 23
Cugnot, Nicholas, 4, 5

Daf (company), 15
Daimler, Gottlieb, 9-10, 11, 12, 20
Daimler, 23, 27, 40, 41
Datsun, 42
de Dion-Bouton, 27
Depression, the Great, 36-37
Detroit, Michigan, 16, 42
Diesel, Rudolf, 8

Dion, Count Albert de, 13
Dodge (company), 29
DUKW, 38
Dunlop, John, 9
Durant (company), 17
Duryea, Charles and Frank, 17

Edward VIII (king of Britain), 22
electric accumulator, 15
electric cars, 15, 39, 47
employment, automobile's effect on, 35
engines: diesel, 8, 46; four-stroke,
  7, 8; gasoline, 10; internal
  combustion, 7; Silent Otto, 8; steam,
  4; Wankel rotary, 46-47
exports, 42, 43

farming, automobile's effect on, 35
Faure, Camille, 15
Ferris (American scientist), 9
FIAT (Fabbrica Italiana Automobile
  Torino), 15, 39, 40, 44
Ford, Henry, 18, 19, 26, 30
Ford Motor Company, 18, 32, 39, 40, 42
Ford Popular, 32
France, 29, 39; early automobile
  industry in, 5, 7, 9, 12
French Grand Prix (race), 14

gasohol, 48
gasoline: development of, 9; shortage,
  39, 41, 42, 43, 48
gears, 12, 29
General Motors (company), 18, 40, 42
Germany, 27, 33, 37, 39; early
  automobile industry in, 8, 9, 12
Great Chicago Race (1895), 17

Guy (company), 23

Haynes, Elwood, 17
Hillman, William, 20
Hispano-Suiza, 29
Hitler, Adolph, 37
Hodges, F. W., 20
Holland, 15
Honda, Soichiro, 42
Honda (company), 41, 42

ignition: electric coil, 11; flame, 10
Industrial Revolution, 4
industry, automobile's effect on, 35
Issigonis, Alec, 40
Italy, 9, 15, 39

Jaguar, 31, 40, 41
Japan, 42, 45
Jeep, 38
Jenatzy, Camille, 15

Kimber, Cecil, 37
Kübelwagen, 38

Lancia (company), 15, 41
Land Rover, 48
Lawson, Henry, 20
Lebon, Philippe, 5, 7
leisure, automobile's effect on, 43-44
Leland, Henry, 18
Leyland, 23, 40
Lenoir, Etienne, 7, 8
Levassor, Emile, 13
Locomobile (company), 17
London General Omnibus Company, 23
Lyons, William, 31

Macmillan, Kirkpatrick, 6
magneto, 10, 29
Malcolmson, Alexander, 18

Marcus, Siegfried, 7
Mark V, 27
Marston, John, 20
Mazda, 42, 47
Maybach, Wilhelm, 10, 11, 12
Mercedes, 12, 13
MG, 37, 40, 41, 43
Michelin (tire company), 9, 14, 39
Model T, 2, 18-20, 25, 27, 30, 31, 40
Morris, William/Lord Nuffield, 25-26, 39, 40
Morris (company), 39
Morris Cowley, 30, 40
Morris Minor, 31, 40
Morris Oxford, 25, 26, 27
Motor Taxation Act (1920), 30

999, 18
Nordhoff, Heinz, 39
NSU (company), 47

Oakland (company), 18
Otto, Nikolaus, 8, 9

Packard (company), 17
paint: color of, 30, 31; synthetic, 29
Panhard, René, 13
Panhard-Levassor (company), 13, 24, 27
Panzer (German war divisions), 38
Paris-Ostend (race), 21
Paris Rouen (race), 14
Peugeout, Armand, 14
Peugeot (company), 39
Peugeot-Citroën (company), 40
Phantom, 24, 37
Plate, Gaston, 15
pollution, 46, 47-48
Pomeroy, Lawrence, 20
Porsche, Ferdinand, 37, 38, 39
Porsche, 47

Pressed Steel (company), 33
Prince Henry, 20, 25

racing, automobile, 14, 17, 21, 36
radio, car, 29
railroads, 35, 45
Ransom Eli Olds (company), 17
Red Flag Act (1865-1896), 6, 20, 21, 45
Reliant (company), 41, 47
Renault, Louis, 14
Renault (company), 9, 27, 39, 47
roads, 33-34, 45-46
road signs, 34
Road Traffic Act (1930), 34
Rochas, Alphonse Beaude, 7, 8
Rolls, Charles, 24
Rolls Royce, 25, 37, 41
Rootes (company), 39, 40
Rover, 6, 40, 41
Rover Bicycle Company, 21
Royal Automobile Club (RAC), 23
Royce, Henry, 24

seat belts, 47
shock absorbers, 29
Shrewsbury, Earl of, 14
Silver Ghost, 24, 30
Simplex (company), 17
Singer, 27
Sno-Cat, 48
South Africa, 48
Spain, 29
speed limits, 21, 23, 34, 41, 48
Spyker (company), 15
Standard, 29
Standard-Triumph (company), 39
Starley, James, 6
steam carriage, 4-5, 6
Studebaker (company), 17
Sunbeam, 20
Sutton, William, 6

Swallow Sidecar and Coachbuilding
  Company, 31
Swallow Sports (SS), 31
Swift Cycle Company, 6
Swimmkübel, 38

Talbot, 14
Talbot (company), 40, 41
tanks, 27, 38
taxis, 22, 27, 33
Thompson, Robert, 9
tires, pneumatic, 8-9, 29
tollbooths, 5, 22
Tour de France (race), 13
tractors, 26, 27, 43
Transport, British Ministry of, 33, 34
Triumph, 40, 41
trolley buses, 35
trucks, 27, 30, 33, 34, 39, 42, 48

United States, 5, 16-19, 23, 30,
  31, 36, 37; post-World War II
  automobile industry in, 39, 40, 42, 43,
  48

Vauxhall Ironworks, 20, 21, 29, 39, 40
Velo, 12
Vickers (company), 38
Voiturette, 14
Volkswagen (company), 2, 37, 39, 40, 41
Volkswagen ("Beetle"), 39, 40

Wankel, Felix, 47
White and Poppe (company), 25
Wilson, Alexander, 20
World War I, 27-28, 29, 32
World War II, 31, 38, 42

Acknowledgments

The author and publisher would like to thank the following for permission to reproduce illustrations:
p. 11 (left) Mercedes-Benz (UK) Ltd; pp. 3, 20, 26 (right) Ford Motor Company; p. 40 (above) V.A.G. (UK) Ltd; pp. 21 (above right), 25, 26 (left), 30, 31 (left), 32 (left), 40 (center and below), 41 BL Heritage Ltd; p. 5 Mansell Collection; p. 6 Associated Book Publishers Ltd (from S.E. Ellacott *Wheels on the road,* Methuen, 1953); pp. 7, 12, 13, 14 (right), 15 (right), 16, 17, 18, 19, 21 (above left), 37 National Motor Museum, Beaulieu; pp. 8, 11 (right), 38, 47 Macdonald and Company (Publishers) Ltd (from R. Wyatt *Cars,* 1971); p. 14 (left) Peugeot UK; p. 15 (left) Fiat and *Quattrouote;* p. 21 (below) Vauxhall Motors Ltd; pp. 22 (right), 23, 35 (right) London Transport Executive; p. 24 Rolls-Royce Motors Ltd; p. 27 The Tank Museum, Bovington Camp; p. 35 (left) BBC Hulton Picture Library; p. 41 BL Cars Ltd; p. 42 Honda (UK) Ltd; p. 44 (left) Fiat Auto (UK) Ltd; pp. 44 (right), 46 Popperfoto; p. 45 David Lee Photography Ltd; p. 48 Pickfords·Industrial Ltd.

Portrait drawings by Ian Newsham
Diagrams by John Blackman
Graphs and map by Jeff Edwards, Marlborough Design
Front cover photograph courtesy of Maserati Import Company. Back cover photograph courtesy of Daimler-Benz A.G.

The Cambridge History Library

The Cambridge Introduction to History
Written by Trevor Cairns

PEOPLE BECOME CIVILIZED

THE ROMANS AND THEIR EMPIRE

BARBARIANS, CHRISTIANS, AND MUSLIMS

THE MIDDLE AGES

EUROPE AND THE WORLD

THE BIRTH OF MODERN EUROPE

THE OLD REGIME AND THE REVOLUTION

POWER FOR THE PEOPLE

EUROPE AROUND THE WORLD

THE TWENTIETH CENTURY

The Cambridge Topic Books
General Editor Trevor Cairns

THE AMERICAN WAR OF INDEPENDENCE

THE AUTOMOBILE

BENIN: AN AFRICAN KINGDOM AND CULTURE

THE BUDDHA

BUILDING THE MEDIEVAL CATHEDRALS

CHINA AND MAO ZEDONG

CHRISTOPHER WREN
AND ST. PAUL'S CATHEDRAL

THE EARLIEST FARMERS AND THE FIRST CITIES

EARLY CHINA AND THE WALL

THE FIRST SHIPS AROUND THE WORLD

GANDHI AND THE STRUGGLE
FOR INDIA'S INDEPENDENCE

HERNAN CORTES: CONQUISTADOR IN MEXICO

HITLER AND THE GERMANS

THE INDUSTRIAL REVOLUTION BEGINS

LIFE IN A FIFTEENTH-CENTURY MONASTERY

LIFE IN A MEDIEVAL VILLAGE

LIFE IN THE IRON AGE

LIFE IN THE OLD STONE AGE

THE LONDON POLICE IN
THE NINETEENTH CENTURY

THE MAORIS

MARTIN LUTHER

MEIJI JAPAN

THE MURDER OF ARCHBISHOP THOMAS

MUSLIM SPAIN

THE NAVY THAT BEAT NAPOLEON

THE PARTHENON

POMPEII

THE PYRAMIDS

THE ROMAN ARMY

THE ROMAN ENGINEERS

ST. PATRICK AND IRISH CHRISTIANITY

THE VIKING SHIPS

Lerner Publications Company
241 First Avenue North, Minneapolis, Minnesota 55401

Texas Poets in Concert

Texas Poets in Concert

A Quartet

UNIVERSITY
OF NORTH
TEXAS PRESS
DENTON

TEXAS POETS
SERIES NO. 2

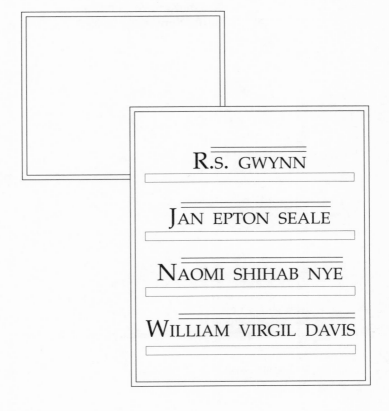

R.S. GWYNN

JAN EPTON SEALE

NAOMI SHIHAB NYE

WILLIAM VIRGIL DAVIS

Texas Poets Series General Editor: Richard B. Sale
Design: Kennedy Poyser
Production: Jessie Dolch

Library of Congress Cataloging-in-Publication Data

Texas poets in concert: a quartet: poems / by R.S. Gwynn [et al.]
Texas poets series: no. 2
ISBN 0-929398-10-6
1. American poetry—Texas. 2. American poetry—20th century.
I. Gwynn, R.S. II. Series.
PS558.T4T39 1990
811'.540809764—dc20   89-21462

Acknowledgments

The authors make grateful acknowledgment to the following publications, in which some of the poems in this volume first appeared.

R.S. Gwynn
Concho River Review: "The Professor's Lot"; *Drastic Measures:* "Yuppigrams"; *NER/BLQ:* "Snow White and the Seven Deadly Sins"; *Plains Poetry Journal:* "The Dream Again" and "Body Bags"; *Pulpsmith:* "The Slave Ship"; *Tar River Poetry:* "Randolph Field, 1938"; *The Texas Review:* "Sir Thomas More"; *The Formalist:* "Approaching a Significant Birthday, He Peruses *The Norton Anthology of Poetry*"; *Key West Review:* "A Letter From Biltmore" and "West Palm."

Jan Epton Seale
New America: "Bandelier"; *riverSedge:* "Coming Down Through Oklahoma"; *Vanderbilt Street Review:* "Digging for the Truth"; *Latitude 30° 8':* "Doing the Valdez Dream," "Nape," and "Rain Dance"; *Aileron:* "Flying Home"; *Calyx:* "In Praise of Woman Chief"; *Gray Sky Review:* "One More for Sylvia"; *Wind Literary Journal:* "Trailride"; and *The South Florida Poetry Review:* "What the Bristlecones Said."

Naomi Shihab Nye
Artful Dodge, Balcones, Bloomsbury Review, High Plains Literary Review, The Madison Review, Painted Bride Quarterly, Pax, Affinities, and *The Georgia Review.*

A number of poems also appeared as part of *The Spoken Page* text/tape project from the International Poetry Forum, Pittsburgh, Pennsylvania, 1988.

"Swimmer, Blessed Sea" first appeared as a broadside by Beck Whitehead, The Southwest Craft Center, San Antonio, Texas, March 1989.

William Virgil Davis
The Akros Review: "Snow" (as "Snow in Ohio"); *Cimarron Review:* "Legacy"; *The Gettysburg Review:* "Windows"; *The Hudson Review:* "A Man and His Hat," "Fragments," "October: With Rain," "Winter Roses," and "Winter Solstice"; *The Montana Review:* "The Light" (from "Six Poems for Georg Trakl"); *The New Criterion:* "Landscape"; *Paris/Atlantic:* "Breton Village in the Snow"; and *Poetry:* "The Polar Bear."

"Winter Light" is reprinted from *One Way to Reconstruct the Scene* (Yale University Press, 1980).

CONTENTS

1   *Introduction*

4   *Body Bags*
Poems and Translations
R.S. Gwynn

34   *Believing Is Seeing*
Jan Epton Seale

76   *Twenty Other Worlds*
Naomi Shihab Nye

106   *Winter Light*
William Virgil Davis

R.S. Gwynn
Body Bags

Poems and Translations

7   Snow White and the Seven Deadly Sins
9   Yuppiegrams
10   Two Songs: From *Notes & Queries: An Academic Opere*
14   Approaching a Significant Birthday, He Peruses
         The Norton Anthology of Poetry
15   A Letter From Biltmore
17   The Slave Ship: A Ballad, by Heinrich Heine
23   Sir Thomas More, by Karl Haushofer
24   The Dream Again
26   Randolph Field, 1938
28   West Palm
31   Body Bags

Jan Epton Seale

BELIEVING IS
SEEING

37   The Specified Donor
39   Digging for the Truth
41   Believing Is Seeing
43   Pilgrim! Pilgrim! Why Do You Tarry?
45   One More for Sylvia
46   Nape
47   Flying Home
48   Bandelier
51   Helping History on Bachelor Hill
52   On the Way to Cinnamon Pass
54   Rain Dance
56   Coming Down Through Oklahoma
58   Kluane Lake
60   Doing the Valdez Dream
62   Songs of Mesa Verde
65   In Praise of Woman Chief
68   Trailride
69   Dear Thunder
71   For Sheep in Transhumance
73   What the Bristlecones Said

Naomi Shihab Nye

TWENTY OTHER WORLDS

79   The Sail Made of Rags
80   Intensive Care
82   Even at War
83   How Palestinians Keep Warm
84   What Brings Us Out
86   Through the Kitchen Window, Chiapas
87   Saved
88   California Time, Texas Time
89   Beyond This World There Are Twenty Other Worlds
91   Sleep's Little House
92   Password
94   Morning Paper, Society Page
95   The Great Photographer Has His Picture Taken
97   Swimmer, Blessed Sea
99   The Edge of a Country
101   The Turtle Shrine Near Chittagong
103   Audience
104   Olive Jar
105   Debris

William Virgil Davis
WINTER LIGHT

109   Fragments
110   Legacy
111   Snow
112   Winter Light
113   Winter Solstice
114   Pathetique
115   The Watchers
116   Landscape
117   Landscape in Early Winter
118   Windows
119   October: With Rain
120   Winter Roses
121   Vigil at *Heiligenkreuz*
122   "Breton Village in the Snow"
123   Winter Stars
124   The Polar Bear
125   A Man and His Hat
126   An Evening in Advent
127   The Light
128   Winter Walk

Introduction

In 1988, poets R.S. Gwynn, Jan Epton Seale, Naomi Shihab Nye, and William Virgil Davis read from their work and conducted workshops at a mini-conference sponsored by the Creative Writing Program at the University of North Texas. This "quartet" of poetic voices is brought together again in this anthology.

The Irish poet Seamus Heany has written that "one perceptible function of poetry is to write a place into existence." The concert of places sung into existence by these four Texas poets is quite diverse, however, and Heany's remarks on the plurality and multiformity of Irish poetry, as well as on the blurred distinctions between who may or may not rightly be called an Irish poet (what about expatriots, for example? visiting or transplanted academics? immigrants?), might also be applied to a discussion of Texas poetry and poets. Accidents of birth, vocation, and the heart have conspired to bring these four poets to Texas from places as far apart as New England, St. Louis, North Carolina, and Waxahachie. And although Texas, as a place, presumably has affected these writers' experiences, the extent of this influence may not be immediately obvious in the work, or even fully known by the poets themselves.

Of the first western pioneers, John Madson has written: ". . . grassland of such magnitude was wholly alien to the western European mind. It diminished men's work and revealed them to a vast and critical sky, and forced people into new ways of looking at the land and themselves and changed the world forever." For our time, I would add to Madson's grassland "shopping malls, mixmasters, and blonde-brick subdivisions of such magnitude"; but nonetheless, we may assume that any place we inhabit in our present, even a place that to us may seem alien, becomes a position or perspective from which to view and understand our subject matter, whatever it may be. Geographical distance, whether proximate or immense, can provide a stance from which a lever can be manipulated to move our past, our desires, our vision — in short, our poems: our imaginative, written worlds. Heany reminds us of the physical fact that asserts that the longer the lever, the less the force necessary "to move the mass and get the work going." At times, he suggests, what is "intractable when wrestled with at close quarters becomes tractable when addressed from a distance." As Naomi Shihab Nye writes, "From a distance/all things can be borne," and born. Texas, then, has provided the present tense or place — at times explicit, at times more subtly felt — from which many of the poems included here found movement and generation. The diversity of subject and form found in these poems is a testament to both individual voices and to the place that lent them perspective and context. "Being alive is a common road," Nye writes, "it's what we notice makes us different."

The turf of R.S. Gwynn's poems — epistolary, dramatic, irreverent, witty, intelligently camp — is one that stakes out the claims and crimes of both allusion (literary, historical) and popular culture in our experiences. This is a poetry of startling juxtapositions, of slaps in the face, nudges in the ribs, and of audacity and even courage. Ever eschewing the sentimental through sardonic wit and craft, these poems nevertheless take emotional risks that shock and move us: "Let the deep twilight gather to the chime/ Of three brass angels," he writes, "circling in the nude,/Tinkling above their candles as they climb/The wall in shadows." And in "Body Bags," Gwynn questions even the power of words to transcend our griefs:

> The piece of chalk
> Splinters and flakes in fragments as I write,
> To settle in the tray, where all the dust is.

Impeccably formed and often musical, these are poems of lyric irony, which Heany says must often take the place of tribal celebration in our time.

Of all the poems included in this anthology, those of Jan Epton Seale perhaps most vividly, and certainly most explicitly, find a literal context in Texas and environs. Her chief interest, though, is in the land as it reveals its people — Native Americans and early settlers, as well as the speaker and her friends and family. In "Coming Down Through Oklahoma," she writes, "The land suffers its history out/in its people"; in "Bandelier," Seale asserts that "there is no change in energy/only people, when they find it, or fail to." Although "the wilderness belongs to itself," human beings are connected by the physical facts of our beginning — we begin inside another. Although the poems address life's losses, they also offer a "yes among old sorrows." The word/world is a mysterious realm, but, Seale asks, "Who says we love least what we do not understand?"

The world of Naomi Shihab Nye's poems is a global village made possible less by technology than by stories, hands, faith. Here are poems of visionary metamorphoses, seemingly tangential at times, but as numinous and revealing as consciousness itself. The poems are empathetic, like the seagull in "The Edge of a Country," who "wore the breath of the whole sea in his wings." And they are generous:

. . . something that might not have happened
had a chance again

You know, that gift we give
to one another

Nye's work gives courage because the questions she raises are the deepest ones. In fact, the reader senses that there is no story, no grief, no path that this poet would not be willing to share, to heal, to transcend. When Nye wonders, "How can we help/Someone else want to live?," her poems themselves are the answer.

The lost or inaccessible worlds of truncated relationships, of childhood, of "the ends of summer," and of the separate body are the real subjects of the poems of William Virgil Davis, their greens and haloes achingly missing in the graphic, abbreviated landscapes. The wintry atmosphere of these poems is that of "the sucked-in breath, held, to make the mind/attentive to the least detail," and the irony of our life sentences is evoked in stark, simple images. What the poems reveal, however, is not static. These are poems very much about change, about the terror that "where summer never ends,/ . . . little changes." Reading a Davis poem is akin, in fact, to waking in a house on the morning of an unexpected snowfall — a subtle change in light and insularity provides a clue to a more immense transformation. Like the terrain of thought itself, these poems disarmingly cross realms (life-death, present-past, imagination-reality), as in "Winter Stars," where the poet's vision of a mysterious, cosmic ice-picker/star-maker causes us to "spin our heads around," to notice, and offers genuine, if chilly, sustenance.

These four voices, then, are diverse, as distinctive as possible, and yet the Texas poets are also bound by their empathy, craft, vision, and a fresh, wry humor. We can be heartened that these four Texas writers have undertaken to voice the conflicts and surprises of our humanity. In "Intensive Care," Nye writes of her sick father and his doctor, a fellow countryman: "at least they shared two tongues,/not one, perhaps this doubled our hope." Fourfold, then, at least, may be the pleasure and understanding afforded by the quartet of tongues joined here.

— *Lisa Russ Spaar*

R.S. GWYNN is the author of the
collection *The Drive-In.* He is Associate
Professor of English at Lamar University
in Beaumont, Texas.

R.S. Gwynn
BODY BAGS

[handwritten inscription] For Michael McFee

[signature]

2 Nov 92

Poems and Translations

For Jason Blair Simon, Dustin Brant Simon,
and William Tyree Gwynn

How with this rage shall beauty hold a plea,
Whose action is no stronger than a flower?

Snow White and the Seven Deadly Sins

Good Catholic girl, she didn't mind the cleaning.
All of her household chores, at first, were small
And hardly labors one could find demeaning.
One's duty was one's refuge, after all.

And if she had her doubts at certain moments
And once confessed them to the Father, she
Was instantly referred to texts in Romans
And Peter's First Epistle, chapter III.

Years passed. More sinful every day, the *Seven*
Breakfasted, grabbed their pitchforks, donned their horns
And sped to contravene the hopes of heaven,
Sowing the neighbors' lawns with tares and thorns.

She set to work. *Pride*'s wall of looking glasses
Ogled her dimly, smeared with prints of lips;
Lust's magazines lay strewn, bare tits and asses
Weighted by his "devices" — chains, cuffs, whips.

Gluttony's empties covered half the table,
Mingling with *Avarice*'s cards and chips,
And she'd been told to sew a Bill Blass label
Inside the blazer *Envy*'d bought at Gyp's.

She knelt to the cold master bathroom floor as
If a petitioner before the Pope,
Retrieving several pairs of *Sloth*'s soiled drawers,
A sweat-sock and a cake of hairy soap.

Then, as she wiped the Windex from the mirror,
She noticed, and the vision made her cry,
How much she'd grayed and paled, and how much clearer
Festered the bruise of *Wrath* beneath her eye.

"No poisoned apple needed for this Princess,"
She murmured, making X's with her thumb.
A car door slammed, bringing her to her senses:
Ho-hum. Ho-hum. It's home from work we come.

And she was out the window in a second,
In time to see a *Handsome Prince*, of course,
Who, spying her distressed condition, beckoned
For her to mount (What else?) his snow-white horse.

Impeccably he spoke. His smile was glowing.
So debonair! So charming! And so *Male*.
She took a step, reversed, and without slowing
Beat it to St. Anne's where she took the veil.

Yuppiegrams

I. Swingers

A singles bar! Warm refuge for the lonely.
Such eager give and take between the sexes
You'd think the action hot. Relax. It's only
The mating ritual of Rolodexes.

II. Dress for Success

Whenas in clinging silks my Julia goes,
Samantha makes a "statement" with her clothes.
What lies within her armored vault of serge
Intrigues me, but I somehow lack the urge,
Imagining gray-flannel, pin-striped lingerie.
A statement? Yes, alas. *Noli me tangere.*

Two Songs: *From* Notes & Queries: An Academic Operetta

I. Terminal Song

Asst. Prof.
>   If you've observed that I have served
>   My term without complaining,
>   Then hopefully it will be me
>   You plan to be retaining.
>   For I'm worn out with dread and doubt
>   And sick of this campaigning.

Chorus of Beards
>   We've heard from you. We're down to two
>   With just one spot remaining.

Asst. Prof.
>   I swear to get the doctorate yet:
>   I've chapters generating.
>   I shall not sleep; awake, I'll keep
>   Revising and collating
>   Until I've made the final grade
>   And finished dissertating.

Chorus of Beards
>   We have one slot. Too bad, it's not
>   For you. But thanks for waiting.

Asst. Prof.
>   Though I lose hair, my grades are fair;
>   I keep a chart for seating.
>   I've published widely on the side
>   And gone to many a meeting.
>   Who could deny a man like I
>   With such a hearty greeting?

Chorus of Beards
>   Your pronoun case is pure disgrace.
>   These words are self-defeating.

Asst. Prof.
>   I'm 42, as old as you,
>   And time is slowly creeping.
>   At night I burn and toss and turn

            While you are soundly sleeping.
        If you had eyes you might surmise
            That I am clearly weeping.
Chorus of Beards
        We note the fact. You have no tact.
            You're not the one we're keeping.
Asst. Prof.
        You'll all regret this moment yet,
            You bunch of hothouse flowers!
        I'll buy a gun. I shan't be one
            To sugar milk that sours.
        I'll plink away your feet of clay
            And pock your ivory towers.
Chorus of Beards
        You'll get your pay, of course, till May.
            Aren't these your office hours?

II. The Professor's Lot

When the student body scorns an education
And would rather sun half-naked on the beach,
Then I sense my academic situation
Is somewhat like a pit without a peach.
Were it just a mid-life crisis I could bear it
But I fear the currents far more deeply run.
There's a lesson to be learned here. I can't share it.
The Professor's lot is not a happy one.
When there's academic duty to be done —
                                    to be done —
The Professor's lot is not a happy one.

Once it seemed the case that a high-school diploma
Guaranteed me students primed for a degree.
Now it means they've spent their twelve years in a coma,
Only waking up to take the SAT.
When I give my class a simple English sonnet
You would think the Day of Judgment had begun.
We could spend the whole semester's time upon it.
The Professor's lot is not a happy one.
When there's academic duty to be done —
                              to be done —
The Professor's lot is not a happy one.

My medieval seminar keeps getting smaller
While the business classes overflow their rooms,
And each year the basketball recruits look taller
But won't qualify for pushing mops and brooms.
Though I'm at a state-supported school in Texas
I affect the accents of an Oxford don
As I say, "My dear," to students of both sexes.
The Professor's lot is not a happy one.
When there's academic duty to be done —
                              to be done —
The Professor's lot is not a happy one.

In my class there is a woman in a turban
Who displays a tattooed lily on her breast.
I could ask her out for chit-chat over bourbon
And let the course of nature do the rest.
But she's probably the type whose disposition
Always finds the dissertation "loads of fun."
Let my sins, Lord, be those mainly of omission.
The Professor's lot is not a happy one.
When there's academic duty to be done —
                              to be done —
The Professor's lot is not a happy one.

On the sad day when I stand before Saint Peter,
He will say, "No extra points. No make-up tests."
Then he'll add, "No need for you to pack your heater.
They've installed a central furnace for the guests."
At the moment when the horny demons find me
I can count this futile struggle halfway won
If the whole Administration's right behind me.
The Professor's lot is now a happy one.
With no academic duty to be done —

to be done —

The Professor's lot is *now* a happy one —

a happy one!

Approaching a Significant Birthday, He Peruses
The Norton Anthology of Poetry

All human things are subject to decay.
Beauty is momentary in the mind.
The curfew tolls the knell of parting day.
If Winter comes, can Spring be far behind?

Forlorn! the very word is like a bell
And somewhat of a sad perplexity.
Here, take my picture, though I bid farewell.
In a dark time the eye begins to see.

The woods decay, the woods decay and fall —
Bare ruined choirs where late the sweet birds sang.
What but design of darkness to appall?
An aged man is but a paltry thing.

If I should die, think only this of me:
Crass casualty obstructs the sun and rain
When I have fears that I may cease to be,
To cease upon the midnight with no pain

And hear the spectral singing of the moon
And strictly meditate the thankless muse.
The world is too much with us, late and soon.
It gathers to a greatness, like the ooze.

Do not go gentle into that good night.
Fame is no plant that grows on mortal soil.
Again he raised the jug up to the light:
Old age hath yet his honor and his toil.

Downward to darkness on extended wings,
Break, break, break, on thy cold gray stones, O sea,
And tell sad stories of the death of kings.
I do not think that they will sing to me.

A Letter From Biltmore

Asheville, North Carolina
February 5, 1905

Two days by rail from Richmond, through a vast
And niggery wilderness, I stand amazed
Before the height of folly: frozen Pisgah
Looming beyond, dwarfed by, so aptly named,
The house, as if in size one might surpass
The visions of one's own ancestors' ghosts.

The weather lays me low, that and the gout
I pray will ease before I travel West.
I limp down endless corridors, not passing
Another soul. I've rung now for the maid
An hour — salts and water. Still have none.
From this high window I can see a pigsty

Tastefully hid by hedge. At least the pigs (I
Can make out six) seem well — *de mauvais goût*
Les plaisirs de cette table. Had I known
Of this unyielding gray that has laid waste
To every charity, I should have made
Connections for less indirect a passage

To Charleston. It is, in the current parlance
(Like Col. Brown, whose rowdy "In a pig's eye,
Dear Mr. Jones," left all of us dismayed)
Too *bully.* I hear of a second guest,
A woman, but alone I make my way
From table to my cell here, seeing no one.

We'll see no sun today. It is just noon,
Time to begin another trek through parlours,
Salons and sitting rooms where treasures wait —
A *room* of Dürers, William, to pass by
And at each turn of hallway make a guess
At which direction may uncharm the maze.

How is it with you, whom this tirade may
Amuse? That one with whom you share a name
(Tho' little else), who never "gets the gist"
Might find himself a slave to passages
That rival his own prose. I warrant, I
Laugh with you here, so fitting is my fate!

The foot may mend tomorrow. Now the pain
Seems part and parcel of a holy quest.
Also, I lack a tooth. Affectionately,
                                    Henry James

The Slave Ship: A Ballad
By Heinrich Heine

The supercargo sits at his books;
His name is Mynheer van Koek.
He totals the bill of lading up
And figures his probable take.

"The rubber's good, the pepper's good,
Three hundred barrels and sacks;
Gold dust is precious, ivory too,
But best of all are my blacks.

"I bought six hundred on the River
Senegal, a steal;
Their skin is tough, their muscles hard,
Like fine, tempered steel.

"I gave cheap brandy, beads and iron
To get them on the ship.
I'll clear eight-hundred percent at least
If half survive the trip.

"If I've three hundred niggers left
In Rio de Janeiro,
I'll get a hundred ducats a head
From the House of Gonzales Perreiro."

Suddenly Mynheer van Koek
Is shaken from his vision:
The surgeon of the ship comes in,
Doctor van der Smissen.

His breathing rattles like a gourd
Through a nose red with warts.
"How be my blacks?" inquires van Koek.
"Come, show me your reports."

The doctor thanks Mynheer van Koek
For his statement of concern;
"Last night," he says, "the death rate took
A sharp upward turn.

"Before, at most, two died a day
But this morning seven were found —
Four men, three women. Here's the log.
I have put my findings down.

"I looked the bodies over well.
These swine will sometimes fake
Sickness and death in order to
Get tossed into the wake.

"Then quickly I unclapped their irons
And called out to the crew
To toss them overboard at dawn
The way we usually do.

"Sharks shop up from the depths at once,
A regular war patrol.
They love this nigger flesh so much
That they are on my dole.

"They have followed closely in our wake
Since we lost sight of land.
The smell of death drifts down to them
And it's more than they can stand.

"It's quite a funny thing, the way
They dine upon the dead.
One holds a leg, one rips the guts,
And one tears off the head.

"And when they're done, they roll about
And loll against the planks
And look at me as if to say,
'Fine breakfast, Doctor. Thanks.'"

"How can we halt these horrors, Doctor?"
Asks van Koek with a sigh.
"What can we do to keep our loss
From mounting up so high?"

The Doctor says, "If they are dying
It is themselves they owe.
The nasty odors of their breath
Have fouled the air below.

"And others die from melancholy.
They're bored to death, I think.
Some fresh air, music and a dance
Should put them in the pink."

Van Koek cries out, "A brilliant thought,
Dear Doctor: Share my bottle.
You are a match for Alexander's
Tutor, Aristotle.

"The president of the Tulipgrowers'
Society of Delft
Hasn't got half a brain as you.
Congratulate yourself!"

"Music! Music! These blacks will make
A dancehall of the ship,
And the nigger who doesn't jump for joy
Will be cured by the whip."

.   .   .

From the firmament on high,
Gleaming large and wise,
A thousand stars shine with desire
Like lovely ladies' eyes.

They gaze upon a sea of silk
Where the waters softly glow
With purple phosphorescent haze.
Waves moan to and fro.

The slave ship lies as if becalmed;
No breezes stir the sails,
But lanterns shimmer on the deck
Where dancing music wails.

The helmsman saws his fiddle bow,
The cooks puff on their flutes,
And the cabin boy beats on a drum
While the Doctor's tin horn toots.

A hundred niggers, women and men,
Dance round and stomp their feet.
They circle wildly; when they hop
Their shackles keep the beat.

They shake the deck with wild desire
And many a beauty moans
As she hugs her naked mate and sweats
To a counterpoint of groans.

The jailer is *maître des plaisirs*
And walks the weaving lines
Urging all to enjoy themselves
With flicks of his cat o' nines.

A fiddle-de-dee, a fiddle-de-dum,
The racket sounds the deep,
And the creatures of the water world
Are shaken from their sleep.

With staring eyes, the sharks come up
To watch, at least a hundred.
They lie just off the teeming deck
And gape at it in wonder.

Seeing that dinner is not yet served,
They yawn and work their jaws
And rip the waves with open mouths
Planted with teeth like saws.

A fiddle-de-dee, a fiddle-de-dum,
The music shrieks and wails.
The sharks, mad with hunger pangs,
Begin to chew their tails.

It seems they don't like music much.
Their cross expressions show it.
Let no such man be trusted, says
Albion's greatest poet.

A fiddle-de-dum, a fiddle-de-dee,
The music fills the air,
And by the mast Mynheer van Koek
Folds his hands in prayer:

"In Jesus' name I pray Thee, Lord,
Their sinful lives to keep.
If they have angered Thee, recall
They are as dumb as sheep.

"Spare them, O Lord, for Jesus' sake,
Who died for us in thunder.
For if three hundred don't survive
My business will surely go under."

Sir Thomas More

By Karl Haushofer

In the Tower, Sir Thomas wound his clock
While peevish Henry, fretting in his bed,
Wrestled with nightmares, kneeling to the block
Beneath which sat a basket for his head.
The King woke sweating, offered one last time
Inducements to that stubbornest of men;
That failing, torturers to force the crime.
Meanwhile, a beard grew from Sir Thomas' chin.

And when they stretched his neck out for the ax
(A stiff, strong neck, all witnesses concurred)
More motioned them aside while groundlings jeered
And calmly said, as if to state mere facts:
"Treason my head committed, not my beard.
Spare it, I pray." That was his final word.

Spandau Prison
Berlin, 1945

The Dream Again

The dream again. Near Christmas. It is time
To lower and unfold the attic stair
That will not hold a grown-up's weight, to climb
Into the chill and naptha-scented air.
Here moth will not corrupt and time must spare
The box of lights and mismatched ornaments
Packed in a carton filled with Angel Hair
And met, as if by sheer coincidence,
With lawn chairs, summer clothes, and two old Army tents.

Mother, an item here belongs to me.
It is a piece of plastic tubing, red
And cane-shaped, which I'll hang upon our tree
In memory of an old man who is dead,
A neighbor on the block I visited
Daily when I was only three or four.
For months I took that thing with me to bed,
Then stopped and did not take it anymore
After he died. I've never known what it was for.

The dream again. We trim the slender tree
With strings of lights so antiquated they've
No colors left, hang icicles and see
These acts reflected, wave on frozen wave.
More rituals: the ribbon that we save
To bind leftover boughs to make a spray
Or two of cedar, handmade gifts you gave
Your parents every year — I watched you lay
Them fresh and fragrant on their tombstones Christmas day.

To make room for the presents we arrange
The furniture and, for amusement, play
Old records that, in retrospect, seem strange:
Gene Autry, Guy Lombardo, Sammy Kaye.
I watch you setting out a metal tray —
Santa drinks Coke — and sing along like one

Who knows what words each character will say,
A sort of *déjà vu*, a knowledge won
From having played the part before, the role of son.

The dream again, the one that always ends
In a light which, while neither cruel nor hard,
Indifferent to my waking thoughts, ascends
In moments made to empty and discard
Like leaves the wind now scatters in the yard.
Yet it is such that I would not confine
It to the space inside a Christmas card
Or the stamped parcels bound with tape and twine,
Sent with regrets for invitations I decline.

So let the light grow dim, allow this dream
Its one still moment, where none may intrude
To hang the stockings which can only seem
Empty reminders of the magnitude
Of love we neither compass nor conclude.
Let the deep twilight gather to the chime
Of three brass angels circling in the nude,
Tinkling above their candles as they climb
The wall in shadows, marking nothing more than time.

Randolph Field, 1938

Hands of men blasted the world asunder;
How they lived God only knew!
If you'd live to be a gray haired wonder,
Keep the nose out of the blue!

Framed by the open window, a lone Stearman
Wobbles, dips right, dips left, then dives and banks
For touch-and-go, seeming barely to miss
The sunlit "Taj Mahal" and a stray egret
That has mistaken grass and shimmering concrete
For salt marsh. Two flies on the windowsill
Wait for their chance. The wind-sock hangs limply
In the thick heat, and lunch is still uncleared.

Indeed, the mess tray resting on the nightstand
Has not been touched, or hardly — half a weiner,
Succotash and boiled carrots stirred around,
Even the tea and gingerbread just tasted,
And the young man there who has no appetite
Has raised himself up from the sweaty pillow
To watch some fledgling's first attempt, as stirring
As a scene from *The West Point of the Air.*

It slips from sight. He leans his head back, dizzy
From the slight effort, shuddering against
The squeal of tires, the buzz-saw radial engine
Over-throttled, straining up to a stall,
And then, the day's sole miracle, the steady
Hum of the prop — somebody else's luck.
For now the chills have come to spike his fever,
Everything holding true to course but him.

The skinny nurse who takes his temperature
Charts the latest, 102.8,
And then connects the dots with a red line
That climbs and plummets like a rookie's struggle
To keep the nose cowl flush with the horizon.
It would be funny, but it simply isn't,
Even when Szulic and Rosenthal, his buddies,
Saunter in after class with Cokes and Luckies.

He'll envy them that night when, after supper,
He lies in bed and smokes. It isn't easy
To think of them with girls along the River —
Dancehalls, music, beer, all with such sweetness
In the mild evening air he'd like to cry.
He has missed the chance, like Aaron Rosenthal,
To burn above Berlin; like Thomas Szulic,
To spin in wingless somewhere over France.

A decade and a war still to be crossed
Before he is my father, he is only
One of the Dodos, barely voting age,
Washed out a week before he gets his wings.
A radio is playing now. Kay Kyser.
. . . *To be in Carolina in the mornin'* . . .
It's hard to think of what he must go back to.
He banked on everything but going back.

Off to the southeast, thunderheads are building —
Heat lightning flashing like imagined guns,
Faint thunder and a breeze that brings the Gulf
Into this place of starched white sheets and Lysol
Where he lies watching three red points of light,
A late flight coming in for night approach.
He shuts his eyes and tries to think of nothing
Before he sideslips into dreams of fire.

West Palm

Arma virumque cano. It should be
That simple, shouldn't it? Sometimes, at night
When Susan and the boys are sound asleep
I'll take my Virgil and the dictionary
And work through lines like these until my eyes
Grow heavy, and I know that I can sleep.
I won't take pills, though Susan says I'm stupid
Not doing so. "You *are* a doctor, Tom.
Write yourself a prescription." But I don't.
The sleeplessness is somehow like the Latin,
Steady and tedious, worth working through.
Arma virumque. Warfare and mankind.

I've known them both and tried to keep my distance.
In '68 I did my residency
At an induction center. Easy work,
Knee-jerks and assholes, Hunter used to joke
When we'd go out to see the daily crop.
Hunter was something else, a hare-lipped sergeant
Who'd done the same routine for twenty years.
I can still hear the way he'd holler out:
"Bend oder, gemmun. Gab you cheeks and spead 'em!"
He'd seen it all, the guys who'd drink raw eggs
For weeks on end to register albumin
In urine samples, those who'd swallow speed
To bring on an arrhythmia. We locked them
Up on the holding ward a day or so
Until their signs were normal and they passed.

I sent so many off to war that year
I can't recall a single face. A scar
Or a tattoo, perhaps, but not a face
Except old Hunter's with his twisted lip
And eyes that cut into me like a scalpel.
We worked on quotas, see. The training camps
Could only take so many at a time
And in those days they called up twice the number
They'd ever use. I'd walk the lines

and feel the kids' eyes on me, almost begging
For me to find some rare deformity
In feet or knees or ears to keep them out.
I guess I had the power of life and death.

I can't remember faces, but I know
I sent some that I shouldn't have, a negro
With tracks on either arm, a pool of pus
Between his feet when he pulled back his foreskin
And stood there grinning at us; a fat slob
With H-A-T-E scratched into his knuckles
And teeth like something from a horror movie.
The clean-cut boys, the ones who answered "Sir"
And seemed to have intelligence as well,
Would get the benefit of every doubt.
Sometimes I'd listen with the stethoscope
Until I half convinced myself I heard
A murmur. Hell, nobody questioned me
As long as every bus to camp was filled.
Hunter caught on, I guess, and hated me
For what I did. He never said a word.
In '69 I got the job I wanted,
Putting the blasted faces back together
And doing what I could to mask the scars.

For years I read of Mengele. Remember?
The Nazi doctor who stood by the trains
And flipped his riding crop to left or right
To send one to the ovens, one to work.
For years they claimed he hid in Argentina
Or some such place. I live in West Palm Beach,
Here in a house my father would have never
Felt better than a servant in — a wife
And two fine boys, a sailboat we could take
Across the ocean if we wanted to,
And a good practice that grows every day.
If Doctor Mengele could see my patients!

Jewish women who beg for better noses,
Larger or smaller breasts or fewer wrinkles.
Ponce de Leon came into Florida
In search of youth. It's here. Pure silicone.

My mother, bless her soul, would keep me up
Past midnight with the tables of declensions
Until I had them down. I could still pass,
With practice say a page of Cicero
So flawlessly you'd think I'd heard the man.
And all these years I've found no use for all
That patience but to help me fall asleep.
I'll go up now and look in on the boys,
My blond and flawless sons who'll help me take
The boat out at first light. We'll catch a breeze
And point the bow out where the blue meets blue
And one soon loses sight of everything.

Body Bags

I

Let's hear it for Dwayne Coburn, who was small
And mean without a single saving grace
Except for stealing — home from second base
Or out of teammates' lockers, it was all
The same to Dwayne. The Pep Club candy sale,
However, proved his downfall. He was held
Briefly on various charges, then expelled
And given a choice: enlist or go to jail.

He finished basic and came home from Bragg
For Christmas on his reassignment leave
With one prize in his pack he thought unique,
Which went off prematurely New Year's Eve.
The student body got the folded flag
And flew it in his memory for a week.

II

Good pulling guards were scarce in high school ball.
The ones who had the weight were usually slow
as lumber trucks. A scaled-down wild man, though,
Like Dennis "Wampus" Peterson, could haul
His ass around right end for me to slip
Behind his blocks. Played college ball a year —
Red-shirted when they yanked his scholarship
Because he majored, so he claimed, in Beer.

I saw him one last time. He'd added weight
Around the neck, used words like "grunt" and "slope,"
And said he'd swap his Harley and his dope
And both balls for a 4-F knee like mine.
This happened in the spring of '68.
He hanged himself in 1969.

III

Jay Swinney did a great Roy Orbison
Impersonation once at Lyn-Rock Park,
Lip-synching to "It's Over" in his dark
Glasses beside the jukebox. He was one
Who'd want no better for an epitaph
Than he was good with girls and charmed them by
Opening his billfold to a photograph:
Big brother. The Marine. Who didn't die.

He comes to mind, years from that summer night,
In class for no good reason while I talk
About Thoreau's remark that one injustice
Makes prisoners of us all. The piece of chalk
Splinters and flakes in fragments as I write,
To settle in the tray, where all the dust is.

JAN EPTON SEALE is the author of two
poetry volumes: *Bonds* and *Sharing the
House.* She also writes plays, essays, and
short stories and lives in McAllen, Texas.

Jan Epton Seale

BELIEVING IS SEEING

The Specified Donor

Mahogany and henna, the sack above my head
like a flask of vintage wine
brings memory of you, hope for me.

At two I doze, despite the plastic
noise around
then start to a mockingbird's song.

Saturdays you prowl the sanctuary
field glasses trained
for groove-billed ani or loggerhead shrike.

Once we shuttled a question between us
for several weeks:
What is a group of hawks called?

Solving the riddle with "kettle"
we've moved on
spiralling in the thermals, with "life"

a vague answer to the new question
unspeakably perched
on the foot of my bed tonight.

Toward dawn I begin on the hospital plan:
L's and H's of floors,
vents, elevators, stresses, exits

while your blueprints for seven projects
hang like clean laundry
on their rack in your office cross-town.

Now the weak light shows rain
against the sealed glass
as uneven and luxuriant as the blood inversely

obeys its precious calibrated drip
on the alchemist's command —
platelets, albumin, plasma descending

like charms. The least I can do
is pray the clouds
harmless to you, gone fishing in Mexico

first giving this tagged present,
premier valentine
with your name in bold marker.

The power surge leaves me with fever,
your blood sending
my blood into a feeding frenzy.

At dawn they take away our connections,
disarm us abruptly.
I move out of mummified pose,

out of the figure imprinted on the sheet,
find I have not for myself
held a wake but a vigil.

The doctor comes, sees you already
teased into my nails.
Now I doze, first sending you

deep in the country, beside the lake
of giant bass
a pink smile, new and only brother.

Digging for the Truth

Raw squirrels and rabbits were his pay
brought to his porch head down,
skins left home for trade.
Never a week went by he didn't
cut a fishhook from a Choctaw's hand.
"Take a big swig of your firewater,"
he'd say, "but leave a little,"
then fetch his quilting thread and needle
and sterilize his knife.
Folks came from miles around
for Charlie Pittman's touch.
He also sang revivals and pulled teeth
but fishhooks were his specialty.

Some say it was because
he had a birthmark on his neck,
not smooth and pink or red
but white and lumpy like a scar.
When he'd inquired, his mother said
he'd started out a frog in the pond,
but Uncle John, fishing one day
had hooked him right there in the neck,
and commencing to skin,
discovered a boy beneath.

He believed the story until he was ten,
told it to his pals and came to be
the laughing stock of Lick Skillet school.

They say he spent the rest of his life
proving people didn't start out as frogs.
The only way to do this was
become an expert in something
where you could dig around for froggy parts
on pretense you were taking out a hook.

When he'd confirmed that they were men
and sewed them up,
he'd burn the hell and tetanus out of them
by emptying the bootleg hooch.
"That's how it burns your guts too,"
he'd kindly say when they got quiet.

He was making sure his mother wasn't right.

Believing Is Seeing

Eyes that have tracked rabbits, birds, deer
all afternoon across the simple oak
now tear and smart, ready as they are
to discover in the cold Hill Country night
Orion among the hot uncompromising stars.

The astronomer emerges from his lens.
"We have a treat tonight," my son says
and waits until a plane has closed its path.
"First you find Orion by his belt."
His finger points me to the spangled girth.

And then we telescope the Great Hunter:
the yellow-red on his right shoulder named
Betelgeuse, a pulsing variable giant,
and Bellatrix on his left; straight down
find Rigel, making his knee a blue-white glint.

We shiver and our breaths form nebulae
of no order. "The next stars" — my son smiles —
"we'll see together. I have to show you how."
I *will* to see beyond the late-night books,
the fog of years, the dimming earthly weather.

"Beside the sword you'll see a cloudy mass."
I strain through waves and jerks from here to there,
search Orion's skirt for starry soil.
The cloud mass finally settles to its place.
"You mean the thing that looks like printers' dots?"

"Orion's Nebula," the astronomer says,
then stands against me firm to make a brace.
"Keep looking, Mom. For now, just blink and stare.
I promise you will see them if you try,
and hope — yes, hope for three bright stars."

Minutes go by. The click of the telescope timer
corrects what we cannot — our restless ride
on this galloping star-drenched porch.
And then the gift: three clear and perfect points,
three diamond apples where none were before.

Afraid to blink, I whisper, "Yes, I see them.
Yes." The astronomer's hand tightens on my arm.
"The Trapezium Cluster, at fifteen-hundred light-years."
He laughs. "I give them to you because you see them."
"I take them," I say, and feel him near.

Pilgrim! Pilgrim! Why Do You Tarry?

Bedclothes will do anything
to trap lovers —
tie them up, hand and foot,
insinuate themselves
into the life of the flesh,
beg to get in the game,
threaten to be winding sheets.

Plates with faces of unkempt children,
cups with seductive lips parted,
forks and knives poking and slicing
at the conversation
hope to win some argument,
tell an anecdote,
get in a word edgewise.

And in the garden a rose bush
pouts for a drink,
an elephant ear strives to listen,
and a tomato plant curls its fists
in fatal threat to the spider mite.

These sly bids for attention
you misinterpret.

For every moan of porch swing,
pillow imprinted with lover's head,
cup of coffee steaming gentle as purgatory,
you hear work calling.
It's order! order! you think
you are called to.

Welts from hot soapy water
rise on your arms like stigmata.
Dirt creeps to your nails
like mice to a pantry.
Dead stems and leaves drape you.

You try to be lost
in conversation
thought
or sex.

You think you can ignore
this itch, this finaggling
of things that love you,
this kind plotting
of your possessions
to keep you out of
the Devil's workshop.

One More for Sylvia

I shut my eyes and all the class drops dead;
I lift my lids and there they are again.
(I wish I'd made them up inside my head.)

I try to make them see that what she said
and what she did were not summarily insane.
I shut my eyes and all the class drops dead.

They drum their pens at babies pickled, tulips red,
list 3 important points on Esther's pain.
(I wish I'd made them up inside my head.)

The boys stretch and see themselves in bed
with girls who haven't poems on the brain.
I shut my eyes and all the class drops dead.

Studying sickies — you sure can't get ahead;
lots of women with kids don't complain.
(I wish I'd made them up inside my head.)

Black stars and rooks and bell jars are too sad.
Poets are nuts. To kill yourself is sin.
I shut my eyes and all the class drops dead.
(I wish I'd made them up inside my head.)

Nape

Here's praise to the nape of the neck,
a much neglected organ. Become a nape watcher

and you see strawberries stamped
at the turnstile of birth; an overhang of hair —

a natural queue, leftover of the widow's peak,
or tail of a valentine, which leads me to say

the nape of the neck is a touch key of love:
feather-stroked, the whole board lights up.

The hair at the nape stays young forever.
Ancients go to their graves black-naped

which leads me to say: when I die,
I'd rather not be redeemed like a gymnast recovering

on a trampoline, springing from grave
to feet blinded by an eastern sun. Rather

let God come like a thick dumb mother cat,
pick up what's left by the nape of the neck,

and move it to safe quarters.

Flying Home

We swim an air-thin ocean in the hearth of a wallow-beast.
We pray our kingdoms come, ourselves to live
when the old leviathan stamps our chests on take-off.

Five miles below, roads excuse themselves
with erector-set bridges over rivers,
gallop alongside trains like B-movie bandits.
From this high, the straighter roads distort,
spike into flagpoles. Swamps become streams,
creeks run to rivers. Trees gather along the banks
for baptismal services until the waterways
fuse in a giant espalier sunning on the wall of earth.

Now the earphones, the hot meals tell us
Jonahs run this whale; drag promises from us
to be reasonable, assure us the pilot's temples
are dabbed that wise gray at the pilot factory,
his blue eyes inserted personally by Santa.

Lowering, we see tidal pools shine
like sliced, wet agates; Padre Island
warms in its lambswool of waves.
Inland, the farmwoman plots her quilt:
pattern of range, cotton, orchard.

We study a metal fin waggling, shunting,
rearranging flow for descent, and farther,
the horizon where, for an instant,
we puzzle which side of the curve we belong.

Small mouths tell us to drink up, buckle up.
Hands snap buttons in the creature's forehead.
We are on schedule. We know the ground temperature.

Suddenly a hum creeps from our throats, a timid song.
Who says we love least what we do not understand?

Bandelier

From Bandelier National Indian Monument
visitors ascend the steep canyon wall to
arrive an hour later in the atomic development
center Los Alamos. — travel brochure

I.
Lichens stencil every stone,
inscribe with rusts, sulfurs, olives

the ways of the great caldera: frozen lava,
water-eaten canyons, wind-carved sandstone gods

lonely for worshippers.
The ruined village Tyuonyi circles,

the kivas safe in their secrets,
the caves above stained with old fires

and drawings of the hunt, speculating
the return of the basketmakers

gone, it is said, before Coronado
because they could not harness

the wind and sky, could not call down
the rains.

II.
North in Los Alamos, lichens
record the isotopes, lasers, reactors.

They micrograve a rock beside the courtyard pool
in the Bradbury Science Hall,

take note of the ballistic cases
posed like two species of dolphin

jumping in the rarified air,
one for Nagasaki, the other Hiroshima.

The sign says: "One of the greatest
scientific achievements of all time."

In one wing the machines Jezebel and Maniac
demonstrate fission and acceleration.

In another, a letter writer named Einstein
tells President Roosevelt a substance

called uranium might be powerful enough
to blow up a harbor.

III.
The guide has just shown the guests
the models of the warheads.

As they stand listening to the difference
in A and H bombs, a boy of eight,
youngest of a touring party,
goes pale and nauseated.

He lies down on the courtyard bricks
as quietly as the photostatic print
of the child found on a step in Hiroshima.

IV.
In White Rock, a town of scientists,
there is a nuclear physicist
growing a garden —
corn, squash, beans
after the calculations each day,
and a row of apple and pear trees.

He waters the asparagus each evening,
his I.D. tags still jingling from his collar.

Sometimes he goes with his children
to a lookout point 15 minutes from supper,
stares down a half mile of lichened boulders
to the river following south toward the canyon
of the starved-out basketmakers.

He thinks of their fission:
the splitting of cliffs;
their project:
earth, sky, and water.
He tells his children
there is no change in energy,
only people, when they find it, or fail to.

V.
The child in the caldera of his mother's lap revives,
ready to walk out into the thin air

past the wall of secret orders,
congratulations to the dedicated physicists.

The physicist is hungry; he calls his children,
descends, checks the water hose before going in.

In Bandelier, the lichens,
without true leaf, stem, or root
comfort the north side of stones.

Helping History on Bachelor Hill

Two saloons and a female seminary are already
in operation and other business houses are expected.
It is to be called Bachelor.

"Creede Candle"
January 21, 1892

Pieces of old glass swim in the tundra,
brittle snow in summer grass:
a sliver of green from a tonic,
an elixir-brown chunk
like tobacco spit on ice,
a square bottom of Price's Delicious Extract.
Here is the lip of a cream pitcher pouting,
there a small congregation of liquor bottle mouths
pursed against the unbearable cold.
With no livers left to cure,
the lapis lazuli blue is just another pretty face.
The cool pink foot of a water goblet
thirsts for a hand to finger it.

Someone says, These bits are useless.
Fragments don't sell.

Someone else says, We know.
Keep picking them up. We're taking in
every little lost rosetta and ticket-holder
of 1892, telling their little cut-glass eyes
and bone-china ears not to worry,
we'll see them through the mix-up.

On the Way to Cinnamon Pass

Once, the mountains staged war,
biting holes in each other.
Now the blood of snows
silvers the gorges
and pines rush down
with a greed of green.
Above the timberline
wildflowers immobilize the world:
scarlet gilia, biscuitroot,
harebell, columbine
weightier than mudslide or snowmass.

What shall we do with this truth?
The deserted mine shafts cry
that if we have a dream,
try hard,
scramble for the lode
we may yet die one night
full of pneumonia,
staring at the tarpaper.

Flowers gamble on the slopes.
Ferns ooze from the clefts.
Lichens in orange and green
mount the slag heaps.
No amount of feet in the world
can trample these moss campion,
penstemon, purple fringe —
no children enough to whiz
these stones across canyons.

The cabins of '92-ers
join the landscape
like deserted beaver lodges,

golden marmots sunning themselves
at imagined doorsteps.
Everything dances
on the downside wind.

Here is yes among old sorrows,
the bleating of lambs
against the first snows
of September.

Rain Dance

It's like this in Texas:
Get your hopes up

over high silver-cake clouds
finally climb out of the pool

go in rejoicing you made it
before the lightning struck

I say rejoicing because
it's still a judgment of God
here in Texas

get dried off and think
of the irony

of being caught in the pool
when the wild thunderstorm hits

on the hottest day of the year.
Bring in the crying dog.

Close the windows at the first
nasty splats.

Thank God that breeze
is coming off the storm cloud

and then nothing.

           It's you're under
the dress of the biggest mamma

in the circus. It's you're
with Poe in the pit.

It's you're in an iron lung
but too healthy for polio.

The clouds, they move
from east to west

always just north of you.
The clouds, they belch a little
like a school boy on request.

The sun, it comes back grinning
like a satisfied lecher.

Cicadas wind up so sly
you don't know what it is

that's winding you up crazy
standing looking out the back door
at where it's not raining.

Coming Down Through Oklahoma

In McAlister there's a big shadow out from town aways
and jailbreaks get first priority on the local station.

Oklahoma City they specialize
in different kinds of crime like
freezing teenagers in meatlockers
and shooting families but not their dogs
on supermarket lots.

And out in the little towns
someone's always torturing a church secretary
or a paraplegic.

Once we saw an 18-wheeler explode
and burn at a roadside park
just north of Red River.
"Something got too hot coming down
through Oklahoma," the man said.

My mother writes from Enid
there was a little boy abducted
from in front of her TG&Y
so be careful in Texas too.

The land suffers its history out
in its people.
The wheat fields seduce the harvesters.
Cantaloupes perfume before they stink,
and oil fields pump books
into new living rooms.

Why do my Scotch–Irish uncles
from Oklahoma look like Indians?

My grandfather writes of the
Indian Territory in 1898,
"Every bridge we came to
seemed to have snakes under it
for which we took a little poison,"

and of his train ride
in the Eastern I.T.,
"Upon looking out the window
I discovered that mountains
were causing the darkness."

They tell us Oklahoma
is getting known all over
for its cancer centers.
It's like the man said,
Something got too hot
coming down through Oklahoma.

Kluane Lake

"No mountain lions in the Yukon,"
assures the Yukoner filling our car,
in reply to the yarn we offer
of a golden something,
big as a calf
with swinging hips and tail
jouncing along the road
in front of us
a half-mile through dense timber.

"Well, maybe ever so often,"
he concedes.

It is the second week in June.
Spring is weak this year.
Rounding a bend, we are shocked
out of forest,
Lake Kluane spread like a giant amoeba.
Water devouring sky.
A conspiracy of silence with space.

We take a long time
wandering down from the car,
careful not to turn an ankle
where permafrost raises the tundra.

Then the music: atonal,
a blur of xylophone and celeste,
maybe shell wind chimes,
a chandelier in a breeze-stoked passage,
a pantry of crystalware in high voice.

Nearing, we uncover the source:
southerly waves stroking a last generation
of ice blocks beached in a cove.
Charmed drunk, we listen a long while.

Finally, the inevitable question:
"If Kluane makes music,
and there's no one around to hear it — ?"

We climb the bank,
leaving the answer for two aged sisters,
who, it is said, live not far from here.
They alone survive a people who spoke
the language called Eyak.

They speak it now
only if they chance to meet.

Doing the Valdez Dream

Where we slept, crabs go about their business.
The grate of our evening fire guards the bay.

Nights I wake at the bottom of Prince William Sound,
feel my body, remember we did not die in the earthquake.

Fact was, we washed our hair,
rinsed away five hundred miles of gravel,
ate salmon for supper and slept deep,
dreaming we were secure after Thompson Pass:
a moonscape, clouds at midday fogging the car,
the boulders colorless as old movies.
"No grass or trees," I record. "Still, a strange sweet smell."
That night the summer huskies guarded our motel,
the earth kept its faults secret —
old glacier above us tawdry with ice melt,
the bay, a dark glass.

Three years later, our bed trawled out of port,
the glacier hard behind, and the huskies,
restless for days before, rode iceberg calves to death.

In the Valdez dream, the '97 panners
cross the glacier toward gold mostly gone.
Their bodies, pink cheeks and all,
appear after decades at the base of the glacier.
They are stored with the respectable dead of Valdez
in lockers, waiting out spring to allow decent burial.

It does no good to say passionately
Tazlina glacier in morning sun
is the road to heaven;
that one should die happy,
having seen the aqua of Worthington's crevasses.
Our bodies themselves are glacial,
slipping in secret year after year,
renewed with fresh sorrow,
pressed flat by tonnage of caprice.

I rise on my elbow in the dark.
"What about us?" I ask when the sign reads:
BE CAREFUL! A CENTURY MAY PASS
BEFORE SCARRED TUNDRA HEALS.

I lie back,
not liquid, not fossil just yet.
Reptile brain transfers
the strange sweet smell
to mammal brain.

Songs of Mesa Verde

I. Little one

I sing for the cups in the rock
    that fit my hands and feet
I sing for the eyes in the rock
    that take me in and out
I sing for the lizard of many horns
    I catch
and the lizard of feathers
    I do not catch

I laugh and thank my mother
    for fixing my head flat
thank my father
    for fixing my house warm
thank the trees
    for sweet water

I say it is good
    to be hot and to be cold
    to ride the turkey
    to swim my hands in the corn
    to make magic in the arms
                of the blue trees

II. Young woman

Never will I stumble
Never will I fall
The new jar of mine
sits on my head
like the nest of a bird

I am the tree
that never falls down
that holds the nest
the nest of corn
the egg of our lives

III. Builder

In my hands is the plan

It begins with the tree
Forgive me tree
I cut you for good use

I lay a tree each way
the wind blows
I lay the stones
in the way of the trees

In my head is the plan

The stones go high as my head
when I make them like fish
with water and earth

The stones rise until they stop
stop when they hear
the crop's song above

In my head is the plan

I make eyes with no-stones
I make a mouth and a tongue
for stepping in and out

We will lie in the stones
when the sun takes his gold

We will lie in the stones
as we lay in our mothers

In my head is the plan

If the place is too great
it will fall down
If the place is too narrow
she and I cannot lie together

In my head is the plan

IV. Old woman

I have not gone out
from this lip of god
for twenty snows
Tomorrow I will not go

I cannot bear the thorns
the sunfire
the heavy way of walking

Tonight my jars are in place
The young ones in my keep
dream their tomorrow

Soon I am a rat
getting into my own store
out of season

Soon I wrap myself
in death skins
I lie down before the great lip

I sing my own death
with a small mouth

In Praise of Woman Chief

Her Gros Ventre mother speaks:

> She was taken from me,
> snatched as she gathered wood.
> She was too young to know
> the ways of men.
> I was not to cry,
> not to go forth for her.
> This was the law.
> But it was not my heart.
> It was not the world
> made for my little one.
> I cried all night in silence for her.
> I asked she be spared the ways of men,
> the death of her innocence.

Her Crow captor speaks:

> I could not violate her
> though I purposed to.
> She did not scream and kick.
> She asked to keep my horse.
> Whoever keeps my god dog
> must be loved.
> I taught her to shoot.
> She rode with me first
> on a raiding party
> when she was twelve.
> Though I say it strangely,
> she became my son.

Her "wives" speak:

> We would have done
> anything she asked.
> She was the magic one of us.
> She needed hide-scrapers.
> She needed lodge-keepers.

We gathered the persimmon
and the chokeberry for her.
We peeled the thistle stick.
She was our mother moon.
We were her four sister stars.

Her companions speak:

The Blackfoot were many.
We were few.
The white man let us
into his fort.
She alone went out
when they signalled
for parley.
We watched with our fingers
like gates before our eyes.
They attacked her
like a buffalo surround.
She shot one dead.
She made two bloody with arrows.
The others turned tail and ran.
In camp, she loved to strike the post
and tell of these coups!

We could not love her in the darkness
like we did other women.
Her touch might have killed us.
Maybe she was a spirit.
Maybe she was a man
in the hide of a woman.
So we let her dance with us,
sit at our ceremonies,
go in to the sacred places.
She was our Joan-of-the-woods
like the one in the French
trapper's tales.

The Gros Ventre chief speaks:

It was an uncertain treaty.
To us, she was Woman Chief,
queen of the Crows.
How did we know
she had come home to visit?
How did we know she was
the same Little Bird
snatched from us
wood-gathering ages ago?
She should have called out
the name of her grandmother.
She should have said words
the French traders taught us.
She should have said
she was home.

Woe unto us!
We have killed
the breath in our mouths.
We have killed our own mother
returning to her bed.

Trailride

In the forest a line of horses
following the stony, root-filled path.
The spirit is everywhere, even birds
afraid to break the silence of deep shade,
not sure if night is oncoming.

The horses are resolute, mythical
in their huge stumblings above the rapids,
always rising out of the dust of switchbacks.
The tiny feet of the white mules
are prayers going about their own saying.

Here is elderberry, there a stone
big as a cabin, spat into these woods
short millennia ago. The aspen grove stands pure
as a lily field, crossing itself against snowslide.
The peaks do not know their names.
They hold last year's snow in the cracks of old hands,
tricks of spring leaking through their fingers.

Now squaw cabbage busies itself in a clearing.
Orange fungus blooms from a stump.
The stinkwort waits in surprise beside the path.
We go forward to go back, looking for something
under the rocks, in the deep of the clear lake,
something handed out by stars.

In the dawn acrid with cold,
the columbines bloom without regard.
Our breath is the only thing not solid here.
The spirit of the land does not need us,
our warm jackets, our laughter.
The sun takes its time on the peaks,
lazy melting butter of day coming on as it pleases.

The wilderness belongs to itself.

Dear Thunder

You were a horse. I dream of you anyway,
how you and I as centaur take the Weminuche trails

until I, slung down, rest under jackpine at dusk,
the lurch of your walk in the pulse of my legs,
until you, freed of your soaked blankets,
shiver and wheeze relief.

The trail boss tells your history:

> I run him into a brush corral,
> left him three-four days,
> snubbed him up to a tree
> one day more. Fifth day,
> on goes the saddle.

> Wild horses,
> they're easier'n
> barn colts to train.
> Wild horses,
> they respect a man.

All day we keep up a friendly quarrel,
I jerking you back from biscuitroot, dandelions.
Those times you win, you eat your fill.
Billie, the white mule, lags with us,
ghost in the underbrush scraping his panniers.

Sometimes it is water. You demand slack rein,
take your time, blow bubbles in the recent snow,
steam rising from your nostrils like a dragon's.

Once, lagging behind, you see the others above
on the quarter-mile switchback,
feel your place in line, take off in a trot
that sends my bones to rhythmic hell and back.
Billie, little coward, scurries rear-guard.

Come morning, I walk a mile for your twelve hundred pounds,
step high through the wet gentians and columbines.

Tonight, years later, I hear your hobbles thumping logs,
see the hump of your mustang nose like a mountain ridge.
Tonight I see the lightning, wait out the interval
before your name. I whisper,

> We were Chiron.
> We were learned in the uses of herbs,
> in soft incantations, in soothing potions.
>
> Thunder me what we were together.
> Thunder me strength, old horse god.

For Sheep in Transhumance

For them to know their sheepness,
the way they make joy, wide miles of them,
the hush after the cry "They're coming,"
dust of the mountain pass sifting forward,
muted clappering of bellwethers, drifting bleats,
puffballs of sky echoing this tsunami of sheep
rushing to silken green uplands,
to brush corrals and snowmelts,

For them, in some sheepish way,
to see themselves change the road to sheep,
the sharp-sided draw go wool:
placid brown eunuchs shouldering along,
their bells, with each trot, loud beards;
the ashen ewes protecting their udders
with constant detour of slate beds,
lambs gaiting doubletime at their sides,

For the dogs to know how their dripping tongues
and toothed grins betray their love of work:
yap, rush, pivot, surprise
working the stumblers and nibblers,
the curious and slow;

For the herder sun-wizened, nostrils pinched,
hair woolly with road dirt, his horse a martian —
to understand the music of his chant,

For the flock spilling upward to cedar and spruce,
down to riverbed, for the hooves' trotting,
each marking its place with scent bag,
for the sheep's faint notion that, beyond force,
they would move for the pleasure of it:
cells of a corporate beast, pulse of musk,
tangle of wool and hair, gleam of hoof and horn.

May no lupine or death camas spring on their hungry path,
no larkspur or horsebrush present a salad.

Let not the liver fluke trace them down
nor scrapie or foot rot or blue tongue follow.

Have the wolf and mountain lion pay calls on each other,
the sudden late snowstorm come another year.

May the herder know the treasure of his long day,
his dogs the blessing of their canine luck,

And make all who have met a sea of sheep
going its way to summer pasture
dream the wonder forevermore
when they count themselves to sleep.

What the Bristlecones Said
(for Bob)

You took me up to see them, bristlecones
you'd discovered the summer before.
They hung, comic and grand, on the edge
of a drop-off a mile down.
Pinus Aristata, endangered species,
a stand or two in six western states,
that's all. At first I wondered
why it mattered, they were so ugly:
gray gnarled trunks suffering from sciatica
or as old dogs trying to scratch themselves,
too many legs and scraggly unsure heads
that would have had dandruff if human,
and should have ducked before the blue spruce.
Still, age and oddness due some respect,
we counted the rings of one, a section
of trunk sawed down (Only Dead Wood Is Taken,
says the sign for handmade ashtrays)
and estimated it was young — 1500 years
give or take a century or two. The odd part —
the trunk is dead; the branches live.
Refusing to come down off their mountaintops,
these stubborn trees make bargain:
they'll look dead, play dead, be sort of dead
in exchange for "home," all the while smiling
in death and birthing little porcupines
glad to snag on anything for a ride
as long as it's traveling higher.
Unbelieving, we touched the branches —
splay of needles with spermy resin
not to leave our fingers for hours,
and the stony lignin trunks impervious to rot
and cool as mummies. A mountain bluebird

perched in the top of one unsaleable pine,
July Christmas angel. In the car,
rain drifting over the high country,
we ate our lunch and puzzled halfway mortality.
We wanted life: dead or alive.
From below, looking back on the grove
sitting smug as buddha, we asked our god
why he was playing favorites.

NAOMI SHIHAB NYE, author of
*Different Ways to Pray, Hugging the
Jukebox,* and *Yellow Glove,* is currently
working on a book of short stories. She
lives in San Antonio, Texas.

Naomi Shihab Nye

TWENTY OTHER WORLDS

The Sail Made of Rags

On a river in Bangladesh, one of the million currents, a
boat with a sail of neatly patched rags is floating past.
A crowd of lean men and women watch it from the shore, murmuring
quietly. Children with bare bottoms leap and dance, carrying
sticks. We stand behind the crowd. Some of the rags are
purple, some tie-dyed — they shimmer in the warm light. I
wish we could stand here a long time and have no one notice
us, have no one imagine we watch them out of pity, or foreignness,
or fear. It is impossible to say to someone, "I perceive in you
a calm which will alter my life forever," and have them
accept it. We are strange, we have buttons on our collars.

Today, miles from their shore, I think of the radiant billowing
sail each time someone mentions "the third world" — where
is the second world, and why are we the first? Maybe the rags
came from old sarongs, were joined by kerosene lamplight, had
been made by the people who stood there. Maybe each stitch
was a blessing or a cry. Maybe there are hundreds of sails
that beautiful and we happened to see only one. Dark shoulders,
billowing breath, from miles away I stand behind you. I look
where you look. The boat is going by.

Intensive Care

The roads to my father's heart
are newly paved.
The man who touched his heart
kissed him on the forehead
as he awakened.
Two men from the old countries,
Palestine, Lebanon,
meeting in such a carefully lit land . . .

A secret comfort to me, outside,
where I was standing and sitting
with women who read *The National Enquirer* all night,
"Infant with a Chicken's Beak,"
generously offering copies to me when through,
that at least they shared two tongues,
not one, perhaps this doubled our hope.

One woman blotted her lips
each time the phone rang
and I leapt to answer,
balanced on the tender pedestal of news.
We hovered by bedsides, gripping, five minutes only:
You, you, you know how to come back,
to reach for the rail.

Beyond those windows
trees resumed their bonier lines.
A helicopter kept lighting on a nearby roof,
blades whirling, soundless. From a distance
all things can be borne.
More than once a wild sun flooded the horizon,
igniting towers, the thousand tiny automobiles
crawling toward offices, paper clips,
crawling, with radio stations casually tuned.

We said everything good we had ever
heard of. Men who sewed their own legs
back on in the fields, who breathed twice
as deeply now. Even the couch sunk in the middle,
startling each new resident,
achieved a storied gleam. And the spaces between us
rose curling into the air like smoke
from that other room of vigilantes
who believed themselves more immortal
than we. The upended stories
and the fierce ellipsis pulsing
in our chests, so when Ricki from Texarkana
said, "The truth is, honey, they *can* die,"
she wasn't talking to us. Not daughters
sisters, not the wife with
a thin blanket folded beside her.
The ones with fists shoved in pockets
strutting past the free coffee machine
repeating Come *on,* Come *on,*
to the silver swinging doors with
electrical connections,
speaking each step and
handing it over:
roads, not roadblocks,
calendars, the kiss that pulls us up
to many many days.

Even at War

Loose in his lap, the hands.
And always a necktie,
as some worlds are made complete
by single things.
Graveled voice,
bucket raised on old ropes.
You know how a man can get up,
get dressed, and think
the world is waiting for him?
At night darkness knits
a giant cap to hold the dreams in.
A wardrobe of neckties with slanted stripes.
Outside oranges are sleeping, eggplants,
fields of wild sage. An order
from the government said
You will no longer pick this sage
that flavors your whole life.
And all the hands smiled.
Tonight the breathing air carries
headlines that will cross the ocean
by tomorrow. Bar the door.

> In memory, Izzat Shihab Idais Al-Zer
> West Bank, Palestine

How Palestinians Keep Warm

Choose one word and say it over
and over, till it builds a fire inside your mouth.
Adhafera, the one who holds out, *Alphard,* solitary one,
the stars were named by people like us.
Each night they line up on the long path between worlds.
They nod and blink, no right or wrong
in their yellow eyes. *Dirah,* little house,
unfold your walls and take us in.

My well went dry, my grandfather's grapes
have stopped singing. I stir the coals,
my babies cry. How will I teach them
they belong to the stars?
They build forts of white stone and say, "This is mine."
How will I teach them to love *Mizar,* veil, cloak,
to know that behind it an ancient man
is fanning a flame?
He stirs the dark wind of our breath.
He says the veil will rise
till they see us shining, spreading like embers
on the blessed hills.

Well, I made that up. I'm not so sure about *Mizar.*
But I know we need to keep warm here on earth
and when your shawl is as thin as mine is, you tell stories.

What Brings Us Out

Something about pumpkins caused
the man who had not spoken in three years
to lean forward, cough, open his mouth.
How the room heaved into silence,
his words enormous in that air:
"I won't . . . be . . . afraid . . .
of my . . . father . . . anymore."
And what silence followed,
as if each heart had spoken
its most secret terror,
had combed the tangled clump
for the hardest line
and pulled it, intact,
from the mass.

I bless that man forever
for his courage, his voice
which started with one thing
and went to many, opening up and up
to the rim of the world.
So much silence had given him
a wisdom which held us all at bay,
amazed. Sometimes when I see
mountains of pumpkins by the roadside,
or watermelons, a hill of autumn gourds
piled lavishly on crates, I think
perhaps this one, or that, were it to
strike someone right,
this curl of hardened stalk,
this pleated skin . . .

or, on an old bureau drawer,
the vegetable-like roundness of a glass knob
that the baby turns and turns
emerging, later, from a complicated dream . . .

the huge navigational face of a radio
which never worked while I was alive
but gave me more to go on than most sounds:
how what brings us out may be
small as that black arrow, swinging
the wide arc, the numbers where silent voices lived,
how fast you had to turn to make it move.

Through the Kitchen Window, Chiapas

Bit by shining bit, the world streams by,
bookbag, broom, even a typewriter passing.
And the men of Zinacantan, faded ribbons
trailing their hats . . .
seconds away from the faces we stare,
baby in his sink, me with boiled water,
stick of soap, amazed by how close we can be
to what never sees us. Here in Mexico
no one pulls a revealing curtain wide.
Quiet days unfurl, center delicate frond of fern,
behind the wall with the bluest stripe.
In the street each morning gathering
shapes from mist, rivers of tightly woven braids.

I placed aside the sprigs of mint
when the woman with the polished twins went by.
Crisp school uniforms blessing the old
as saints must bless the breath of sleep,
and the man with stump and rag-wrapped head
shining briefly, Chamulan women leaning forward
in a cloud of mutterings, woolen dolls
stuffed somewhere in their shawls.
Blue, black, each mouth a slash of red.
And the small wafers of episode repeating,
neighbor girl who held the gate
while the freshly shaved Señor
backed his car onto narrow cobbles.
Huge lock echoing in stone.

For this I left my home and made another home.
They were kissing, the lovers, pushed up
against the brightening wall.
His hand followed the tangled trail between
her waistband and blouse.
They were pushing pulling up the hill toward
school and work and uncles.
They were planted on the road and
they were all alone.

Saved

Once I burned a man's letters
in a metal can in front of him

a wisp of that smoke returns
in the clear breath of mountains
his rueful look   the flare of anger
that struck the match

nothing we'd planned to happen did
we have all been saved so many times

why I should think of this
years later in such elegant air
not wondering what happened to him
or feeling regret but thinking instead
how the signs on abandoned motels
west of Langtry Texas have faded more
each year

EXCELLENT BEDS
just a pale red whisper now
TILE BATHROOMS
ghost of a promise
receding into stucco wall
SLEEP WELL HERE

California Time, Texas Time

Knowing you are always two hours ahead of me
that you have risen and showered while I was
placing my slow dream hand on the faces of things
stone bench   bark of eucalyptus
as if to carry them in a pouch beneath the skin

knowing you move into streets
while I curl under the blanket
while birds in olive trees
are sending out their tiny mists

that before I read the headlines
you have read them
have placed the cup to your lips and swallowed
feeling the warm streak in your belly
is like being with you on the trail again
you always ahead of me pressing back branches
saying "Let's go!" when I fell into
my weird staring moods

now you bridge the slash of mountains between us
you send out an hour you are finished with
I live it again and pass it west
as if waves were waiting for it
somewhere inside the drift of sky and sea
a fish is turning so slowly
the hour wraps around him and he shines
not even knowing it and dives deep

Beyond This World There Are Twenty Other Worlds

My friend spreads deer corn
on her son's grave
she wants deer trailing up
from the stream and bowing there
the pointed press of their feet

how long the list
what we'd like to believe

in my boy's favorite word book
a raccoon wears trousers
talks on the telephone
nightly we greet him
name the sacred trilogy
fire   lightshade   raccoon

I don't tell how his chickens
vanished from the coop
why we still find stunned feathers
in the grass

at her house we lean toward the floor
wanting to pick things up scrap of ribbon
wanting a clue   what to do next
at our house we are always scrubbing
removing fingerprints   rubbing with rags

this was Daddy's beautiful shirt
he says sorrowfully   this was Daddy's
beautiful underwear   I have ripped off
buttons and elastic   he smooths
the little squares

we will arrange the pictures on the table
one behind another
to show somebody growing up
go back far enough to find Alaska
the bedsheet printed with rabbits
go forward to a season of many pauses
how we paused ladling soup because
she had just said his name   the phone suspended
between rings because no one could
reach

Sleep's Little House

What an open mouth this hour has

all night among netted leaves
I walk reaching for you
far down the path   arms growing
as I walk   as the branches snag
my shirt

near the hidden logger's bridge
reclaimed by trees   saplings springing
from its mossy span   we found
a small mountain of drinking glasses
buried up the bank from the stream
and most of them not broken

if we went far enough on this road
we would probably come to huts
a tumbled shack   a roof
they had to stop cutting sometimes

sometimes I feel you going deeper and deeper
into the growth   the secret farther forest
more than what I say waited to be said
but the needles brushing my cheek
the sinking sponge beneath us
more than what anyone could say
had already lived here and fallen

in the book of bears
a little house holds a little bed
the bear notices when his quilt is rumpled
he recognizes the difference in his spoon
when it has been used by someone
he doesn't know

Password

I have made so many mistakes
you might think I would sit down

Here when it rains the streets
forget themselves
A woman swirls away in her Italian car
and the whole city mourns
She could sing, they say
till her voice inscribed the stars
and something that might not have happened
had a chance again

You know, that gift we give
to one another

How can we help
someone else want to live?
The man who sprays trees
stands beneath his hose
bathing in poison
a mask gets in his way

Here the roses stay on the branch
till sun steams their petals like blackened collars
they smell burnt when I pick them
I knew a shirt-presser with a rag on his head
who said "Hung-over"
as password into each new day

I have missed him, strangely
missed the evenings we walked among train tracks
writing old crisscrossed messages in the weeds
how vacant I felt
sister to melancholy
even the strangest parts of ourselves
growing dear

A child awakens crying for candles
those little tiny skinny ones he says
meaning incense sticks
he wants to clutch them in his bed

I have slept so many times
you might think I would really be awake
by now

Morning Paper, Society Page

I can never see fashion models,
lean angular cheeks, strutting hips
and blooming hair, without thinking of
the skulls at the catacombs in Lima, Peru.
How we climbed down from blurred markets
to find a thousand unnamed friends smiling at us
as if they too could advertise
a coming style.

The Great Photographer Has His Picture Taken
For Manuel Alvarez Bravo

Against the wall he leans, impeccably still,
patience of stucco wearing itself into
soft ridges, one white glove.
Above the patio, clouds breathe
their softest evening song,
fluted wings brushing the distant
streams of jets, while the younger man
arranges his camera, turns knobs
on tripod, kneeling, and the great photographer
waits. I could imagine a smile here
wide as the smile of any history repeating,
but the photographer's wife appears
to videotape the man taking the picture,
the baby falling down in leaves,
and me. Also the dusty papier mâché bulls
in the corner. Her camera is so new
it can watch its own film.
The baby hands scraps of red stem
to the photographer, who whispers
Gracias! or El Otro!, wanting to
take them, wanting not to move.

Here the wrapped bell rings.
The hum of attention shines vividly,
pitched. I wish to stay where blue
is really blue long enough to figure it out.
Dreaming what will filter down into baby,
cradled deep with breast and fanning palm,
reclining woman wound in gauze —
on the table, prints we have known
for years, resting, at home.
We have followed a great man in
to the light that separates fingers,
strands, from the crowded body of days.
He has said This, and This, his voice

soft as cirrus, as the bellies of ducks
scrambling in the garden.
Later his wife will see these moments
winding backwards in the tiny window
as another fist of hours softens into night,
and the street accepts three more people,
washed with silence, filled with eyes.

                          Mexico City, 1987

Swimmer, Blessed Sea

*"Well, when his head is clean off and its
riddance is enjoyed, what are the likely
results for the headless one, in the light
of the past decade's experience?"*

D.E. Harding
On Having No Head

1.

Once pregnant women looked at me
as if I had forgotten something.
I wanted to rap my knuckles
against cribs, flannelette bathrobes,
the meanings of names.
They stood on the edge of an ocean,
poised and confident, arms raised.
The rest of us were just getting older.

2.

Now the world echoes with cries of children.
Blue shirt, front cash register, he says his name is Ray.
Now I join the federation of those
who entered days tired and could not lie down.
My mother with pony tail and plaid dress
pulling us to the grocery in a wagon —
probably we whined or wished for something,
her arm ached, and for sure it was uphill.
Once, walking home, a milk carton
burst in her arms. Milk streaming —
her pale, pale eyes. I join the shadow
at table or sink, the leaning, lifting self
that answered, "Yes?" a million times.

3.

When you lived inside me I was a boat.
Rising, twirling, you steered me toward the bed
for naps.
I rode those days carefully,
seeking smallest waves.

You raised the flag of a new country in my heart
and all its citizens ran out to greet us
when we arrived.

4.

I love you, hymn and hymnal,
battering oar!
An owl lights your room at night.
I want, I need, immediate bloom.

Now grandfathers stoop
at the grocery store,
touching your fat feet
to their foreheads.

To pregnant women I say *Sister,*
to Self I say *Wait.*
Here is the second story,
telling you more.
This door that opened,
this window that cut off my head.

The Edge of a Country

"What does it matter
if my lips have been sealed?
I have put a tongue in every mouth
of my chain."   —Daud Kamal

I.

At a party, he stooped, spoke his name
so quietly an hour later you learned
whom you were speaking to.
Mountains of rice loomed between us,
whole ranges, and the difficult pass,
till finally an arching bridge
was found. He was throwing stones in
from a high place. He was shielding his eyes.

Once, on a night drained of electricity
near the Khyber Pass, I stepped on a prayer rug
without praying, and a gasp went up
the length of the room. We visited refugees
with stony eyes, we drank their bitter light
and bowed. *Buy this rug in memory of a country*
which will never be the same, blaze of reds
in the sun. They told of the bomb shaped
like a doll, so children would lose their hands.
"To shatter the morale of the parents," — and I closed
my books and papers for days.

From the broken well,
crumbled windowframe,
darkest path where foxes padded,
their feet weavings of delicate bones, a voice:
"You know how the dailiness remains
all we have, luxury of days, they fight
so they can have this?" Till he took the silent page
and opened it.

II.

Friend, to learn you died in a Macy's store
does not fit. Traveler gathering gifts,
the sky of New York should have lifted you clear,

winged you home. I think of the gray suit,
chalk-dusty, thin, the thinness of your paper,
and the long-drawn pause you held
before speaking any line. Your student confiding,
"We are servants to his words."

Today in the yard one iris sings
a coming wheel of sun. Behind the museum
mossy steps rise from the ground.
When my class described them, some wrote
they headed down, and others up.
I descend to the valley of roots,
pressing cool syllables to my lips.
Buddha-stone, wrote one boy, and the echo
of your country, *Ensha' Allah*, returned.
Each day woven into our rooms,
stringed peppers, loom of light,
the drum of news throbbing beneath it,
knot of tears unleashing its shine.

III.

My friend whose father died
is greeted by monarch butterflies
wherever she goes. I followed her,
forgetting, till one flashed across our path
burning a yellow hole.

Each birthday our doubt grows
slightly older. Our cargo of surprise,
our chain. Because you lived,
lives grew to the edges of many countries.
The gull which paused for a moment
this morning, on a pole near the Pacific,
wore the breath of the whole sea in his wings.

The Turtle Shrine Near Chittagong

Humps of shell emerge from dark water.
Believers toss hunks of bread,
hoping the fat, reptilian heads
will loom forth from the murk
and eat. Meaning: you have been
heard.

I stood, breathing the stench
of mud and rotten dough, and could not feel
encouraged. Climbed the pilgrim hill
where prayers in tissue radiant tubes
were looped to a tree. Caught in their
light, a hope washed over me
small as the hope of stumbling feet,
but did not hold long enough
to get me down.

Rickshaws crowded the field,
announced by tinny bells. The friend
beside me, whose bread floated and bobbed,
grew grim. *They're full*, I told him.

    But they always eat mine.

That night I told the man I love most
he came from hell. It was also
his birthday. We gulped lobster
over a white cloth in a country
where waves erase whole villages, annually,
and don't even make our front page.
Waiters forded the lulling currents
of heat. Later, my mosquito net
had holes.

And all night, I was pitching something,
crumbs, or crusts, into the bottomless pool
where the spaces between our worlds take root.
He would forgive me tomorrow.
But I wanted a mouth to rise up
from the dark, a mouth, hand,
any declarable body part, to swallow,
or say, *This is water, that is land.*

Audience

Always one man reeking of salt
"just off that ship" he waves, wild glint
of seaspray sharpening his eye

Or the Texan who sprawls
in the back row, man with tight hips
who drove fifty miles, sleeps in a barn
and asks me to sign someone else's book

Always they lean toward that whine of wind
beyond the door
And what I could have brought them
haunts me

Hands, dangling
these three small stones

Olive Jar

In the corner of every Arab kitchen, an enormous plastic container
of olives is waiting for another meal. Green tight-skinned olives,
planets with slightly pointed ends — after breakfast, lunch, each
plate hosts a pyramid of pits in one corner. Hands cross in the
center of the table over the olive bowl. If any are left they go
back to the olive jar to soak again with sliced lemon and oil.
Everyone says it was a good year for the trees.
At the border an Israeli crossing-guard asked where I was going
in Israel. To the West Bank, I said. To a village of olives and
almonds. To see my people.
What kind of people? Arab people?
Uncle and aunt, grandmother, first and second cousins. Olive-
gatherers. Do you plan to speak with anyone? they said. Their
voices were harder and harder, bitten between the teeth.
I wanted to say No, I have come all this way for a silent reunion.
But they held my passport in their hands. Yes, I said. We will
talk a little bit. Families and weddings, my father's preference
in shoes, our grandmother's love for sweaters. We will share
steaming glasses of tea, sweetness welling in our throats. Someone
will laugh long and loosely, so tears cloud my voice: Oh space of
ocean waves, how long you tumble between us, how little you dissolve!
We will eat cabbage rolls, rice with sugar and milk, crisply sizzled
eggplant. When the olives come sailing past at dinner in their little
white boat, we will line them on our plates like punctuation. What
do governments have to do with such pleasure? Question mark.
Yes I love you! Swooping exclamation. Or the indelible thesis
statement: It is with great dignity we press you to our lips.

Debris

A woman phones to say she found two of my poems
in the parking lot at the university. "They were
in a parking space," she says, "all damp and messy.
For some reason I stopped to pick them up. Do
you want them back?" I tell her I haven't taught
at the university in two years, they must have
dropped from someone's notebook, thanks for noticing,
and what are they, by the way?

A week later I'm out front watering oregano plants
and a thin bearded man hesitates across the street.
A little girl is with him, carrying letters. They
cross over and he asks my name, then says he found
one of my poems in the gutter in front of this house
a few days ago and has now grown fond of it. "It
must have fallen out of your trashcan," he says,
pointing to the very spot where we place our cans.
"It was about India." He offers that a few lines
were crossed out, so I know it must have been an
earlier draft of a recent poem. Do I want it back?
We shake hands and he goes off with his radiant
daughter.

Later I think of these two unexpected readers and
feel grateful for their downcast eyes as they walked,
strolled, as they went about their daily business.
I think maybe I should lose more things: surely
there are more ways to publish than we have heard
of, more ways to make a living, stay awake. Even
today almond trees are snowing white petals across
the road to my grandmother's village and the men
who walk through them, the men and women who walk
through them, sometimes step gently and sometimes
pause.

WILLIAM VIRGIL DAVIS's collection
One Way to Reconstruct the Scene won
the Yale Series of Younger Poets compe-
tition in 1980. Currently Writer-in-
Residence at Baylor University, Waco,
Texas, he is also author of *Understanding
Robert Bly*, a critical work.

William Virgil Davis
WINTER LIGHT

For Carol and Bill

"The mind is the great poem of winter"
— Wallace Stevens

Fragments

At first you think you are still asleep
but the light in the opened window burns
your eyes and the wind has blown the curtain
over the high-backed chair and knocked
the fragile porcelain to the floor. The
fragments lie scattered like fallen flower
petals. This must have been what wakened you.
You lie alone and stare, in this room you
have for only the week, in this place
you never dreamed to be, and think how
strange it has all become. Beyond the window
the steady wind and waves wash the ends
of summer through all your waking thoughts.

Legacy

In winter, when wind huddled the house,
when snow fell deep and slow, we'd wait
to hear our breath translated back to blood,
trace it all out, over again, an endless
sentence, as if we never knew, hadn't heard
it all before. Sometimes, nights like this,
we remember it again and pile the years,
and burn them back like calendars.

Snow

In early fall it fell over everything.
The eye of the pond would suddenly
blink shut and stay closed all winter.

The stiff corn stubble froze, snow
fences for field mice. The barren trees
in the small woods, with snow along

their limbs, were like painted post cards
we could keep or send. This was where
we grew. Now the years come and go

and there is no way to account for them.
Memories blur, but I have not forgotten.
This is my mind of winter.

Winter Light

All night through the dark the dark
is falling. Dead limbs fill with water,
freeze in the hard light of winter.

Out walking this early morning, I stop,
stoop, stare at my own reflection,
bent like a branch is bent by water.

Winter Solstice

A pink wash over everything
and the wind down to whisper.
Squirrels stop on bare branches
and blend in so quickly if you look
away you never find them again.

This twilight must happen only
here, only once or twice each year.
I saw it first last winter, black
trees and houses lined up along
the horizon like silhouettes cut

out of paper and set up along
a board in a classroom long gone
into memory, where I first stared
at the shapes light makes on things
and learned I wanted to repeat them.

Pathetique

Such a hush, ends and beginnings. All day this music
named me. My ears eyes. It is winter again but there is
no snow. The small house is empty, the wine chilled,
Italian, the bread hard, good, the cheese old, the apples
firm and tart, the best this season. Outside, I watch
the small lake settle through slow mist, still, rising.
It takes me away, the way memories call across long
distances, rehearse all the old terrors. You know, my
brother, what I remember, but I have been waiting here
alone for many lonely years, hoping to tell someone.

The Watchers

The clear bell of the window,
struck by sun, burns clean.
All the edges hold,
this moment, without wind.

Branches pile with new snow.
A single bird, black, holds
against the slate gray sky.
Even the air still, stopped.

This window has worn
the eyes thin, the winter
light burned deep within
my mind. Years turn

and turn again. How old
we are. The window breaks,
falls from the frame.
Last light rings the dark hill.

Landscape

How old the dark has become,
standing silent in these fields while
horses weave through each other's shadows.
They have come like warm rain
and run over the hills in the moonlight
and stood so long alone no one
impatient would ever notice them there.

When the wind and the winter return
the horses will still be here,
their silhouettes outlined in the pale moonlight,
standing still and silent on these hills
or stamping, splattering snow in small spills,
the whole scene turning slowly into landscape
like our own earliest memories.

Landscape in Early Winter

The clouds open their coffins
and dark comes down
like the final curtain.

Before morning it will rain
or snow. All the lines
gone wrong.

Do not wait awake
unless you understand
the ways of wind and weather,

unless you remember
the only way out of the cave
under the cliff at high tide.

Windows

The light on the apple is a small window
reflecting the room. In it
I see you staring out over the mountain
covered with first snow.
Here, where summer never ends,
where the world is flat, little changes.
Nothing without notice. I know
you would understand such attention
to detail. I remember you said
you had memorized the mountain, the route
you would take to the top, step
by step. I imagine the snow falling
and you sitting beside your window,
waiting for the precise moment
to begin. When I turn to the window
behind me, only my face reflects
in the fading light.

October: With Rain
for my son

The way the light lasts longest on a single spot
of windowpane, some small distortion in the glass
that keeps its final clasp of wind and rain as well,
has caught my eye again. My son has grown so fast
toward man I marvel my own age, try to sort out all

the years, run the film as far forward as I dare.
We sit together at the table, this wintry day with rain,
and do not speak, although I think we think the same
things out, muse on the rain and windowpane,
and in our own ways try to fill the final outline in.

Winter Roses

November: the cold walks stark
in sunlight; the whole hillside
filled with snow. On the small
balcony, you stand and stare.
Your coffee cools in the tiny
china cup beside the marble
balustrade where winter roses
bloom in heated glass containers.
The fragile curtains frost
with fresh designs. It is all
years ago now. You stand alone
and see how unobtrusively
the dark fills up the dark.

Vigil at Heiligenkreuz

The cold comes close around us,
breathes with me.
Do I drowse? In the corner,
near the cracked column,
a young monk slips past so quickly
I almost miss him.
He is late, hurrying to service
with his brothers.
He does not think to look
over his shoulder,
never would have noticed me
sitting half-asleep in the long dark
down the cold aisle
of the centuries
where we both serve.

"Breton Village in the Snow"
(Gauguin)

It would be warm
under those covers.

The place is pure
contentment,

watched by eyes
of houses over

the slow hills.
See how the fences,

bushes, broken
steeple, fail

to follow any
form but their own.

Winter Stars

The night sky is pockmarked with the white ice
they are. They spin our heads around, seem
to stare back at our stares. All's still. The air
a sucked-in breath, held, to make the mind
attentive to the least detail. It is as if the sky
were one huge silk cloth, ice-picked by a gloved,
hidden hand, the only sign of it the quick glint
near the dipper reflecting from the silver handle,
the thin blade put already hastily away.

The Polar Bear

Surfaces from under ice,
glides to the icy shore.
Everything here is white,
absence of all color.

Tests the crust of ice
with his paw, breaking
the edges away, once, twice;
and then begins hauling

himself out of the water,
shedding chunks of ice.
Stands and shakes water
from his fur in white

light. Leaves a track
anyone can follow.
Here the only thing dark
is death. Dark and brittle.

A Man and His Hat

Once, in winter, half the world away,
I watched a man chase his hat over
a mountain of snow. The wind carried it
continually ahead of him and he ran
through blown snow as if in slow motion.
He would almost reach it, then the wind
would catch it again and lift it off ahead
of him. He ran and ran but the wind kept
the hat out ahead of him. He climbed through
fences, around bushes, through fits of wind
and swirling snow so that, sometimes, I
lost sight of him. But always the hat
blew off ahead of him until finally I saw
him stop, sit down in the snow to rest,
watch, while his hat blew on and on
until it rounded the mountain and was gone.

An Evening in Advent

The moonlight has lifted the water from the well.
Along the long road every pebble shows, grows whole.
The corn stubble still stands in its even rows.
Each tree can be seen individually. Everything's still.
This is the kind of night, when we walk out alone,
that we feel blessed, even among our own shadows.

The Light

It is the most white light.
The dark, like a drawer, has slid shut.
We wait and the nothing happens.

There is no beginning or end.

The key has turned tight and locked.
The mirror on the bureau burns.
We wait and we wait again.

Winter Walk

The dark comes early.

All afternoon a light snow
fell. Now the moonlight

runs her smooth hand over the land
and the wind whispers above it.

The small sound of my going
reminds me how close

above the dark we go.